A New Guide
to the
Palace of Knossos

A New Guide
to the
Palace of Knossos

by

LEONARD R. PALMER

FREDERICK A. PRAEGER, Publishers
New York · Washington

BOOKS THAT MATTER

Published in the United States of America in 1969
by Frederick A. Praeger, Inc., Publishers
111 Fourth Avenue, New York, N.Y. 10003

© 1969 in London, England by L. R. Palmer

Library of Congress Catalog Card Number: 78–76551

Printed in Great Britain

Contents

Illustrations

PLATES

TEXT FIGURES

Illustrations

Preface

Year by year thousands of holidaymakers and cultural pilgrims flock to Greek lands and waters to view the many sites which bear witness to the ancient civilization that flourished during the Aegean Bronze Age in the second millennium B.C. Among the archaeological sites the palace of Knossos in Crete has long been accorded pride of place by both scholars and tourists. To the many who wish to increase their enjoyment and understanding by serious preparation this book is addressed.

A new *Guide* has become necessary because of the researches stimulated by the decipherment of the Linear B tablets which were found in such abundance at Knossos. It has gradually become clear that the monumental account of his excavations written by Evans in the *magnum opus* of his old age (*The Palace of Minos*) is distorted by errors of fact. This was pointed out by the Italian excavator Professor Doro Levi in 1958 but the extent to which this took place did not become apparent until the excavation records kept in the Ashmolean Museum, Oxford, and in the library of the British School at Athens had been carefully studied. Moreover, correspondence with his excavator Duncan Mackenzie has brought to light that even at the time of the excavations at the beginning of the century Evans had imperfect control and knowledge of the operations and that at least on one important occasion he made a communication to an international congress without having seen the material in question.

Study of the records has made it possible to make the necessary adjustments to the published accounts. That the time has come to present the new results and conclusions to the general public is suggested by a change which has come over the scholarly scene. While many professional scholars understandably have found themselves unable to contemplate the drastic change in the archaeological and historical picture, the man most directly concerned, Mr M. S. F. Hood, who was Director of the British School at Athens in 1960 and immediately came forward with a vigorous defence of Evans's factual statements, after study of the new evidence has publicly acknowledged that the overall picture of the facts presented by myself is correct. The whole hypothesis of the 'squatter' reoccupation of the palace site Hood declares to be a myth invented by Evans to explain away the masses of late pottery which did not fit into his historical thesis. It is clear that the Linear B tablets are contemporary with the late vases with which they were associated.

The task of submitting the evidence to visitors to this important site is all the more urgent because of the great changes it necessitates in accepted accounts of Aegean history during the Late Bronze Age. As E. Vermeule, author of *Greece in the Bronze Age*, has recently written, 'One cannot arbitrarily declare a set of objects to be LM III B rather than LM I, in rough terms to move them from the early fifteenth to the late thirteenth century B.C., without threatening the whole historical fabric so painstakingly worked out on dozens of sites in the course of the last eighty years.' The magnitude of the upset may be acknowledged. But this *Guide* does not attempt any arbitrary declaration. It merely sites the said objects in the positions in which they were found as opposed to where Evans said they were found. That this is disturbing for those who rely on stylistic dating is understandable. But they may find food for reflection in the tragi-comedy of the Throne Room frescoes (see p. 68).

This *Guide*, after a brief introduction sketching the archaeological framework and the scientific problems involved, takes the visitor through the palace quarter by quarter. The route is marked by arrows on Plan I. At each key place the excavation results, as ascertained from the new sources which supplement and correct the published accounts, are presented. Plans, figures and plates summarize the evidence. Emphasis has been put on the famous works of Minoan art since these are the focus of interest for the tourist. Finally, the Appendix takes the visitor rapidly through the Knossos exhibits in the Archaeological Museum at Herakleion, with references to the discussions in the

Preface

body of the book. Some notes have been added for the guidance of scholars, junior and senior, who wish to break through the barrier of the handbooks and devote themselves to the long overdue task of verifying the facts for themselves.

My thanks are due, once again, to the Visitors of the Ashmolean Museum for permission to consult the Knossos archives and to members of the Department of Antiquities for the assistance they have given me in my researches. The photographs reproduced in Plates I, II, and IV come from this source. I am indebted to M. J. Raison for supplying the photographs for Plates II and V. The drawings for the figures and plans were done by Miss Christine Court, with the exception of those taken from the excavations reports—Figs. 1, 8, 10, 13, 19. For permission to publish these I am grateful to the Management Committee of the British School at Athens. Dr S. Alexiou was helpfulness itself during my many visits to the site of Knossos and to the Museum of which he is the distinguished Director. Last and not least, I owe a debt of gratitude and affection to Sinclair Hood. Throughout this long and often heated dispute he has been a model of scholarly detachment, courtesy and good temper. I owe much to the stimulus of the many discussions we have had. He seeks, of course, to save Evans's date by reclassifying the late pottery which prompted Evans's invention of the 'squatters', but so far this has met with firm rejection from his fellow archaeologists. Time will show.

Worcester College,   L. R. Palmer
    August 1968

Introduction

'The excavation of the Palace of Minos at Knossos is one of of the most important historical events of the century.' Thus wrote J. D. S. Pendlebury in the preface to his *Handbook to the Palace of Minos* (1933). Pendlebury meant 'archaeological events', of course, and his statement is no exaggeration. In fact, the outline of Bronze Age history sketched out by Sir Arthur Evans on the basis of his excavations at Knossos at the beginning of this century has remained substantially unchanged even in the most recent and authoritative accounts, e.g. the revised edition of the *Cambridge Ancient History*, at present in progress of publication.

The history of the Aegean during the second millennium B.C. may be viewed as a struggle between two cultures, the Mycenaean culture of the Greek mainland and the Minoan culture of Crete. The former was the discovery of the German Heinrich Schliemann, whose imagination had been fired as a boy by the ancient Greek tales about the siege and capture of Troy. Homer tells how King Agamemnon of Mycenae mustered a great force of ships to avenge the wrong done to his brother Menelaus of Sparta, whose wife Helen had been abducted by the Trojan prince Paris. In his description of the Greek forces in the second book of the Iliad, Homer gives us a detailed picture of the Greek world in this Heroic Age. The potentates included, besides Agamemnon and Menelaus, such famous figures as Nestor, whose palace was situated at Pylos in the western Peloponnese, and Idomeneus of Knossos in Crete. In the nineteenth century classical scholars were inclined to regard the Homeric stories as pure fiction, but Schliemann firmly believed in their literal accuracy. So, after amassing a fortune, he went in search of the palaces and cities which figured in the ancient stories. To the consternation of many professional scholars he uncovered the site of Troy, the palace at Mycenae, and much else besides. A particularly notable event was his discovery of the unplundered Shaft Graves at Mycenae with their rich grave gifts and the gold death masks which are displayed in the Archaeological Museum at Athens.

Schliemann firmly believed, of course, that he had found the tombs of the Homeric kings and he telegraphed to the King of Greece to announce that he had gazed on the face of Agamemnon. The 'experts' of his day reacted vigorously, and his finds were variously interpreted as remains left by Celts, Goths or Huns; others attributed them to Carians, to Byzantines or Scythians, anything except Bronze Age Greeks. But further archaeological work stimulated by Schliemann's amateur genius gradually filled out the picture of the high civilization which is now called 'Mycenaean' after its main centre. Starting, according to present computations, around the beginning of the sixteenth century B.C., this civilization reached its acme during the fourteenth and thirteenth centuries and came to an end towards the close of the twelfth century B.C.

A scientific revolution was brought about by the work of Arthur Evans at Knossos. Schliemann had also been attracted to Knossos because of its great prominence in the Greek tales, and he had planned to dig there; but he found the price demanded by the Turkish owners too exorbitant. After Schliemann's death in 1890 Evans was more successful in his negotiations. Having acquired the site, he started excavating in 1900. By 1902 he had uncovered the greater part of a palace which yielded astounding artistic treasures. Simultaneously an Italian team was excavating the site of Phaestos, some thirty-five miles to the south. What came to light in these two places were the elaborate palaces of an old culture far exceeding the Mycenaean in sensibility and sophistication. To this culture Evans gave the name 'Minoan', after the King Minos who in Greek legend was the son of Zeus and grandfather of Idomeneus, the Homeric king of Knossos. The splendour and brilliance of the Minoan civilization were such that Evans became convinced he had found the cradle of the Mycenaean culture of the Greek mainland. Gradually he came to regard

Introduction

Mycenaean simply as a colonial version of the Cretan culture. Even after the final destruction of the Minoan palaces of Crete towards the end of the fifteenth century B.C. the Minoans, so Evans believed, transferred themselves to the Greek mainland and carried on from there. Thus the great period of Mycenaean culture was also credited to his 'Minoans'.

Evans gave firm scientific shape to this view of Aegean history. He was one of the first to see clearly that for the purposes of history as a 'before-and-after' account, the most important part of archaeological evidence is pottery. Pottery styles have a limited life, and history as written by archaeologists is in essence largely an account of the distribution of successive pottery styles. In using pottery as historical evidence the archaeologist is guided by two commonsense principles. First, the date of the latest *occupation* of a building is given by the pottery found on its floors or in the destruction debris. Thus Evans dated the final destruction of Knossos from the pottery which he classified as Late Minoan II. This is the so-called 'Palace Style' (see Fig. 4). Secondly, the date for the *construction* of a building is indicated by the latest type of pottery found in 'sealed deposits' below its floors or incorporated in the masonry of its walls or under their foundations. Naturally, a site like Knossos must surely have been exposed, after its destruction, to all kinds of disturbances; and these may have introduced into the deposit misleading later material which archaeologists call 'intrusive'. Consequently, in an extensive site like Knossos it is the overall picture which counts, and particular significance attaches to finds from below pavements and other such solid floors and to material found inside wall masonry and under wall foundations, for here the suspicion of 'intrusion' is minimized.

The succession of pottery styles which is translated into historical succession should be guaranteed by stratigraphy. Ideally, as the archaeologist digs down through the layers of a site that has been occupied over a long period, he hopes to find different styles of pottery clearly separated by distinct horizons, such as floors. Evidently, if such a series can be established, the lowest layer will be the earliest. Little satisfactory evidence of this kind, as we can now see, was obtained at Knossos. But the Italian excavators at Phaestos have been more fortunate. There, after the frequent earthquakes which devastated the island, the Minoan builders covered the ruins of the palace with a layer of concrete to obtain a level for rebuilding. Such stratification has provided indisputable evidence that there had been no fewer than three phases of reconstruction of the 'First Palace' at Phaestos, while the 'Second Palace' was built above the ruins of the third phase of the First Palace with a different orientation.

Despite the lack of clear stratigraphy at Knossos, Evans divided the 'Minoan' pottery into three successive ages, and each of these ages he subdivided into three. In this way he devised a chronological framework: Early Minoan I, II, III; Middle Minoan I, II, III; Late Minoan I, II, III. Evans's *système de classification* was subsequently applied to archaeological finds on the Greek mainland, where scholars determine the chronology by reference to a series of pottery styles called Early Helladic, Middle Helladic, and Late Helladic, again with subdivisions. The Late Helladic period is also known as 'Mycenaean'.

Evans also determined the absolute chronology for the pottery styles. This he believed himself able to do thanks to a series of fortunate finds. At Knossos he found a number of Egyptian objects to which Egyptologists could attach an absolute date, and he stated that certain of these objects were associated with one or other of his pottery styles. Thus he reported the find of an Egyptian statuette inscribed with hieroglyphs datable to the XI or XII Dynasty. He said that he had found it 70 cm below the pavement of the Central Court at Knossos in a widespread pure stratum of pottery, classified as Middle Minoan II B. This is one of the key facts of Aegean chronology, and scholars still rely on this statement as evidence justifying the conclusion that the beginnings of Middle Minoan II B pottery can be assigned to the first half of the eighteenth century B.C. (e.g. *The Cambridge Ancient History*). However, study of the early reports and the excavation records have shown that this statement is inaccurate. The statuette was found on the pavement[1] and *not* 70 cm below it, while Evans's own notebook[2] reveals that his test pits in the Central Court at this point yielded material from below the pavement as late as Late Minoan III.

Using this succession of pottery styles with their apparently

Introduction

secure chronological anchor-points, archaeologists have sketched the following outline of Aegean prehistory (see Chronological Table I, p. 133). The Greeks, according to this account, invaded the Balkan peninsula at the beginning of the second millennium B.C. This migration was merely one episode in a great movement of peoples speaking Indo-European languages who spread out from a centre located somewhere in South Russia. At much the same time, or perhaps a few centuries earlier, speakers of another Indo-European language group ('Anatolian'), which includes Hittite and Luvian, were moving southwards into Asia Minor. The Greeks founded the settlements known to archaeologists as Middle Helladic, and it is from their characteristic pottery that scholars determine the date of entry as about 1900 B.C. For long the Greek intruders remained quiescent in their new abode, gradually consolidating their position. It was not until about 1600 B.C. that they came under the influence of the high civilization of Crete, the rise of which is likewise dated to about 1900 B.C., although some experts argue for a date some two centuries later.

After the Greeks had thus come into contact with the 'Minoans' of Crete, the course of Aegean history is the story of a more vigorous and warlike people supplanting those from whom they had learnt the arts of civilization. The Minoans of Crete seem to have remained dominant in the Aegean until the fifteenth century B.C., engaging in widespread commerce. During the latter half of that century, however, they were challenged by the new 'Mycenaean' power which had grown up on the Greek mainland. The climax came when all the major sites of Crete were destroyed. Knossos itself, which had sometime previously secured dominance over the other Cretan centres, fell about 1400 B.C., and thereafter Crete lapsed into poverty and isolation from the rest of the Aegean. In the words of a leading authority, Crete became for centuries an island without a history. From about 1400 B.C. for about two hundred years the Aegean was dominated by the Mycenaeans who occupied much of Crete (but not Knossos!) and other islands, including Rhodes and Cyprus. They made their influence felt as far as Asia Minor and Egypt. Finally, during the thirteenth century B.C., the Mycenaeans themselves were threatened by enemies who included in all probability the ancestors

19

of the later Dorian Greeks. About 1200 B.C. all the major sites of Mycenaean Greece suffered disaster. The Mycenaean world lingered on for something like a century. In the eleventh century there begins the Dark Age from which the Hellenic world emerged in the eighth century B.C. It is this account of second millennium history which is now challenged by facts recently made available, and it needs to be fundamentally rewritten (*cf.* Chronological Table II, pp. 134–5).

2. The Growth of Doubt[3]

What is peculiar about this story is the position of Crete in general, and of Knossos in particular, during the period after 1400 B.C., when all the major Cretan centres had supposedly been destroyed. During the acme of Mycenaean power and, more appositely, at the time of the Trojan War, in the days of Agamemnon of Mycenae, Menelaus of Sparta, and Nestor of Pylos, Knossos, in Evans's version of history, had long been a ruin, the haunt of 'squatters' who had reoccupied such parts of the site as offered shelter. Yet a great many reputable Homeric scholars continue to believe that the epic reflects with reasonable accuracy the historical picture of the Late Bronze Age. How, then, does Idomeneus of Knossos, dominant king of a flourishing Crete with its hundred cities, fit into an archaeological picture which presents Knossos as 'deserted except for the ghosts of its departed glory, mournfully wandering down the empty mouldering staircases, the silence broken only by the crash of falling column or block', and Crete as 'an island without a history'? Despite this oddity, the great majority of archaeologists have assented, and still assent, to Evans's version of Cretan history and reject Homer. The only point of dispute which arose was the time at which the Mycenaeans intervened at Knossos.

Evans was firmly convinced that Knossos remained the abode of non-Greek Minoans until its final destruction about 1400 B.C., and in this he was supported by a great weight of informed opinion. However, there was a minority view, powerfully argued by the Englishman A. J. B. Wace and the American C. W. Blegen. It seemed to them that much of what Evans had reported from

Introduction

Knossos in his late Minoan II period (dated to 1450–1400 B.C.) bore a marked resemblance to products from the Greek mainland. They suggested, therefore, that during this final period, when Knossos dominated the whole island, it had been the residence of Mycenaean Greek kings who had captured it from the Minoans. A long and bitter dispute broke out between the 'islanders' and the 'mainlanders'. The views of Wace and Blegen remained those of a small minority of scholars until the decipherment of the Linear B script by the young English architect Michael Ventris in 1952.

This brilliant feat inaugurated a truly Copernican revolution. It first showed that Evans was entirely wrong about the occupants of Knossos during the time of the Last Palace. Then, further study of the newly deciphered documents disclosed so many anomalies in Evans's historical picture that doubts previously expressed by certain archaeologists about the accuracy of his excavation reports were reinforced. These doubts led to a scrutiny of the excavation records, which had been deposited after Evans's death in 1941 in the Ashmolean Museum at Oxford to make them available to scholars. To anticipate, it may be said that virtually all the key statements in Evans's chronological scheme are in conflict with his records.

What were these tablets, the reading of which has produced such far-reaching effects?[4] Evans had been led to Crete in the first instance by his researches into Aegean scripts. He had convinced himself that so complex a civilization as the Mycenaean could not have been illiterate. From 1889 on, when an inscribed four-sided bead was presented to the Ashmolean Museum, where Evans was Keeper, he went in pursuit of other such evidence. By 1893 he was able to communicate his discovery of an Aegean system of writing distinct from the Hittite and the Egyptian. Gradually it became clear that this script had a history: a first stage of conventional picture writing had been succeeded by another in which these signs had been simplified to linear outlines. Two phases of this linear script were distinguishable: Linear A had been followed by Linear B. Evans noted that most of the inscribed objects which he had been able to trace in all probability came from Crete: here was the cradle of Aegean writing. In 1900, when he began to dig at Knossos, his deductions found brilliant confirmation. Almost immediately, close to the surface, he began to find quantities of clay tablets inscribed with the characters of Linear B. The finds continued as he excavated year by year, and virtually every quarter of the huge building yielded up evidence of such bureaucratic activity. That the deposits had remained undisturbed since the great fire which had destroyed the palace was evident from the fact that the tablets often formed coherent sets and lay close to the surface in a deposit of carbon ash. Sometimes even remains of the boxes were found along with clay sealings showing traces of the cord with which the boxes had been fastened. Evans never published more than a small selection of the tablets, and as a consequence scholars were unable to tackle the task of decipherment. However, in the meantime great discoveries were being made on the Greek mainland.

Evans was convinced that a similar form of writing must have existed in the palaces of Mycenaean Greece, despite Schliemann's failure to discover tablets at Mycenae and Tiryns. Evidence which substantiated the correctness of this deduction gradually accumulated. A jar bearing characters having some resemblance to Linear B signs was found at Orchomenos, and similar vessels turned up at Mycenae and Tiryns. In 1921 no fewer than twenty-eight such inscribed jars were found in a magazine of the Mycenaean palace at Thebes. But it was not until Blegen's excavation of the 'Palace of Nestor' at Pylos in Western Messenia in 1939 that clay tablets closely resembling those of Knossos were found in a mainland palace. After the war, when excavation was resumed, Wace followed up this important discovery by unearthing some Linear B tablets from burnt houses outside the fortification walls at Mycenae. Later, a few very charred specimens were unearthed in the citadel itself. Quite recently, a few fragments have turned up at Thebes. The Linear B script thus appears as the system of writing used by the Mycenaean Greeks. It is significant that in Crete Linear B has been found only at Knossos.* At the other sites Linear A was used, as it had been at Knossos before the advent of Linear B. Ventris's decipherment of Linear B demonstrated to the

---

* Since this was written LM III B sherds inscribed with Linear B have been discovered at Khania (the ancient Cydonia) in West Crete.

satisfaction of most philologists that all these Linear B archives were written in an early dialect of Greek.

For the Mycenaean palaces of the Greek mainland this was no more than had been expected by philologists. But now Knossos presented a series of puzzles. The long dispute over the occupancy of the 'Palace of Minos' during the Late Minoan II period (1450–1400 B.C. according to Evans) was now apparently decided in favour of the minority opinion propounded by Wace and Blegen: the rulers had evidently been Greek. But in the light of the new evidence a 'final destruction' of Knossos in 1400 B.C. appeared odder than ever. We now had the paradox that the great period of Mycenaean expansion in the Aegean was inaugurated by a great Mycenaean disaster in the island which holds a strategic position in the Aegean. During the two hundred or so years that followed the all-powerful Mycenaeans were excluded from Crete and from Knossos in particular, where apparently 'squatters' presented the sole obstacle to its recapture.

The archaeological story of West Crete was also seriously out of joint. It has long been held, and recently reasserted in an authoritative work[5] on the last phase of Mycenaean history, that the western part of the island was not settled until after the destruction of Knossos. In particular, Cydonia, a site near Suvla Bay and the modern town of Khania, is said to have first been founded in the Late Minoan III B period, that is the thirteenth century B.C. That this was a settlement by Greeks is suggested by an interesting philological fact: Cydonia stands out among Cretan place-names as a Greek formation; it means 'town of the Cydones'. But if both archaeologists and philologists agree in making Cydonia a foundation of the Mycenaean Greeks of the thirteenth century B.C., how can we explain the fact that Cydonia is mentioned repeatedly in the Linear B tablets from Knossos allegedly written in the fifteenth century B.C. ?

Again, the mainland jars inscribed in the Linear B script presented a further puzzle. Once the tablets were deciphered, it turned out that many of these jars had words written on them which occurred as Cretan place-names in the Knossos tablets. The resemblances were so complex that the possibility of coincidence appeared to be ruled out. It looked as though these jars had been exported from Cretan places under the control of Knossos. Recently the Cretan origin has been confirmed by chemical analysis of clay samples taken from some of the Theban jars.[6] Evans dated all these inscribed mainland vases to the Late Minoan III B period, and this date has been confirmed in the most recent study by a French expert. Here was another strange discrepancy. How could Crete, allegedly ruined, impoverished and isolated, be exporting luxury goods like perfumed oil (for that is probably what these jars contained) to so many palaces of the Greek mainland some two centuries after the supposed final destruction of Knossos?

The veteran excavator Carl Blegen voiced archaeological doubts stimulated by the decipherment.[7] Thanks to Ventris we can see that the Greeks of Knossos dominated much of the island. They were in a position to say which shepherd had how many sheep at numerous sheep stations scattered throughout Crete. This implies that the Knossians had close control and effective communications. Blegen, for his part, wonders how so complete a conquest could have been effected 'without leaving visible traces of violence and damage to the Palace itself'. So much for the beginning of the Greek seizure of Crete. But how to explain the devastating fire that destroyed the palace at the end of its occupation by the Greeks? And after it, why did the Mycenaean Greeks tamely abandon the site to defenceless 'squatters', though they ranged far and wide in the Eastern Mediterranean? Did the great potentates who launched an expedition against Troy find themselves unable to cope with the revolt of Minoans on their doorstep and yet build themselves a complex residence at Hagia Triada in the south of Crete?

In 1958 Blegen published an article suggesting that the Linear B tablets of Knossos were more or less contemporary with those of Pylos and that the 'Last Palace' had been reconstructed by Greek dynasts in the thirteenth century B.C. Attention was now focused on the evidence which Evans had offered for dating the destruction of the palace at Knossos. Close scrutiny of his successive stories revealed so many contradictions that it seemed advisable to check his statements against the excavation records, which fortunately could be consulted in the Ashmolean Museum at

Introduction

Oxford. It is now generally admitted that the elaborate stratigraphic picture which Evans had offered as his sole 'decisive
evidence' for dating the tablets was a total fabrication.[8] Not one
of the objects assembled to devise the convincing picture of
archaeological evidence was in fact found anywhere near the
room where Evans located them at their several stratigraphic
levels (see below, p. 76). Similar doubt attaches to almost every
key point of the canonical *système de classification* first published
by Evans in 1905. The eminent Italian scholar Doro Levi, the
excavator of Phaestos, has gone so far as to say that in the
archaeology of Bronze Age Crete we must wipe the slate clean
and start all over again from the very beginning.

Not only has it been shown that there were serious inaccuracies
in reporting the archaeological evidence from Knossos, but doubt
now attaches to the very basis of the historical accounts. Scholars
have acted on the belief that the styles Late Minoan II, III A,
and III B represent a chronological succession. In fact the majority
even hold that it is possible to make a precise chronological distinction between such minute subdivisions as LM III A: 1 and
LM III A: 2; and they would place the destruction of the Palace
between LM III A: 1 and LM III A: 2. But it now appears that
LM II, LM III A and LM III B were all in use simultaneously.
Such is the finding of Sinclair Hood, formerly Director of the
British School at Athens and a leading British authority on
Knossos. Hood has justly observed[9] that 'the reoccupation by
squatters at Knossos is a myth invented by Evans and his assistant
Duncan Mackenzie' and that the Linear B tablets and the associated clay sealings were found in the same destruction debris as all
these different pottery styles. It is true that Hood has proposed
to reclassify the 'reoccupation pottery' as LM III A. This
proposal has, however, not found acceptance, and it seems that
we must follow Levi and concede that all is now in the melting
pot. The following sketch of Aegean history during the second
millennium B.C. is offered as a tentative working hypothesis (cf.
Chronological Table II). The evidence for the later part, when
Knossos was supposedly inhabited by 'squatters', will emerge in
the course of our tour of the site. There it will become abundantly
clear that Hood's statement of fact is correct: the deposits of

tablets and the associated sealings were found together with the
Late Minoan III B style of pottery, which Evans attributed to
his 'squatters'.

3. THE NEW HISTORICAL PICTURE[10]

Shortly before 2000 B.C. an invasion of Asia Minor took place
by people speaking a group of Indo-European dialects known to
scholars as 'Anatolian'. The Hittites settled in the northeast,
while the Luvians, who spoke a closely related dialect, occupied
the south and west facing the eastern Mediterranean and the
Aegean. There is some evidence, hotly disputed, that the Luvians
also occupied the Greek mainland, introducing such place names
as *Parnassos*.* They may also have been the people who built the
first palaces in Crete, which on the new low chronology are datable
to the eighteenth century B.C. The Greeks invaded the Balkan
peninsula in the wake of the Luvians, and their arrival at Mycenae
may be marked by the building of the great fortification walls
there and by the erection of the 'beehive' tombs (i.e. the tholos
tombs such as the 'Treasury of Atreus'). They also occupied the
western Peloponnese, and this invasion may perhaps be associated
with the building of the Palace of Nestor at Pylos. This was first
constructed at a fairly late date (1300 B.C.) and was destroyed
roughly a century later. The decisive expedition against Knossos
was not launched until this late period. There is abundant
evidence stratified below palace floors and inside the masonry
of the walls to show that the Last Palace at Knossos, the Linear
B Palace, was built after a fire which took place within the Late
Minoan III B period. In other words, the history of the Last
Palace at Knossos parallels that of the Palace of Nestor at Pylos.
This gives firm archaeological support to Blegen's suggestion
about the last phase at Knossos, namely that it was the work of
Mycenaean dynasts contemporary with those of the mainland
palaces.

The seizure of Crete was a major episode of the Mycenaean
expansion in the eastern Mediterranean. The Late Helladic III B

---

* E. Laroche, a specialist of unquestioned eminence in the field of Anatolian
philology, has reached this conclusion.

period (1300–1200 B.C.) was the time of their ascendancy, but towards the end of that period they went down under the on-slaught of other Greek tribes speaking the Doric dialect. These invaders came from the north, so that the mainland palaces were first affected. The islands of the Aegean had a period of grace. Its length is difficult to estimate with any precision, but eventually the Dorians also took possession of Crete and Rhodes. This was the situation when 'Hellenic Greece' re-emerged into the light of history after a Dark Age during which the arts of civilization declined and even knowledge of writing was forgotten. Our revised history is thus first a tale of the struggle of Greeks with 'Luvians' and then a clash between Mycenaean and Dorian Greeks. Knossos reflects this in its archaeology. The Last Palace, with its Linear B archives written in Mycenaean Greek, stands above a 'Penultimate Palace', which yielded some specimens of Linear A tablets. The Penultimate Palace was Luvian; the Last Palace was Creto-Mycenaean, and its destroyers were the Dorians. In Hellenic times during the first millennium B.C. the Greeks of Crete spoke a dialect of Doric, but it was largely suffused with elements from the speech of the Mycenaeans they had subjugated. There was no century-long gap between the expulsion of the Mycenaeans and the advent of the Dorians. The Mycenaeans became the serfs of their Dorian conquerors. Historians have noted that even some elements of the social organization of the Mycenaean Greeks survived.

4. THE PROBLEM

The visitor to the site, faced with such profound differences of scholarly opinion, may well ask how far it is within his competence to judge. He may be reassured. The issue is one of the greatest simplicity and it requires no technical competence whatsoever. Did Evans find an Egyptian statuette in A.D. 1900 on the pave-ment of the Central Court or 70 cm beneath it? In 1913, when, as he told us, he carried out his test pits in the Central Court, did he find a widespread Middle Minoan II B stratum, or did he also find Late Minoan II–III sherds? All the points raised in the bitter dispute about the 'date' of the construction and destruction of the

Introduction

Last Palace at Knossos boil down to such simple questions of physical location. How can such issues be decided? None of the present disputants can claim to have been an eye-witness to Evans's operations in 1900 and the following years when the evidence was obtained. This means that any scholar who claims 'to know the facts' must support this claim by citing some written source.

No archaeologist would simply trust his memory for the find circumstances of the enormous mass of pottery and other objects retrieved in excavations of such magnitude and long duration. An excavation without meticulous records would be a waste of time unless it is conceived purely as a treasure hunt. Evans did in fact make careful preparations to ensure that his excavations were competently observed and recorded. In her *Time and Chance*, a biographical sketch of the life of Sir Arthur Evans, Dr Joan Evans has written that the Scot Duncan Mackenzie was employed because he had great experience in keeping the records of an excavation. He had previously kept the Day Books of the important British excavation at Phylakopi on the island of Melos, which lies about half-way between Crete and the southern tip of Attica. The editor of the report of that dig expressly states that it was based on the Day Books of Mackenzie.

The point must be stressed because an excavation destroys evidence in the form of location as it removes objects from the ground. If find position is all-important, then there is no appeal against the testimony of the record written at the time when a given object was found and removed from the soil. An object in a museum case or a sherd in a box is by itself not archaeological evidence. As Seton Lloyd, formerly Director of the British Institute at Ankara has stated, in archaeology the scholar is dependent for his interpretation on the setting in which an object is found. As regards Knossos, this means that if the dig was entrusted to Mackenzie, as was certainly the case, we have no alternative but to rely on his recorded observation of find positions. If doubt is cast on his reliability and competence, this affects not only the excavation evidence from Knossos, but also from the British dig at Phylakopi. How much Evans relied on Mackenzie is plain not only from his explicit references to the Day Books but also from

his frequent verbatim quotations from the excavator's pottery
notebooks and pottery analyses.

This brings us to the collection and registration of the all-
important fragments of pottery. This basic archaeological
evidence, which forms the foundation of present accounts of
Aegean prehistory, was again the work of Mackenzie. Evans
stated in his report for 1905[11] that he had organised a reference
museum of sherds from the whole excavation. The baskets of
sherds from the various floors and levels had been carefully
arranged and labelled by Dr Mackenzie. Eventually, this collection, with later additions, now housed in the Stratigraphical
Museum at Knossos, was studied and published by J. D. S.
Pendlebury, who became Evans's assistant in 1928. Pendlebury
himself dug a number of supplementary test pits. As we shall see,
the evidence he obtained is of great importance.

One other person concerned in the technical recording of the
excavation must be mentioned. This was the architect Theodore
Fyfe. Fyfe was responsible for drawing the plans published along
with the excavation reports. It is a symptom of the growing
difficulties in which the defenders of the orthodox position find
themselves that they have not only questioned Mackenzie's
accuracy but also the competence of Fyfe. It has been asserted
that there were serious inaccuracies in his plans. However, this
move prompted more diligent search in the Ashmolean Museum,
and it turned out that Fyfe's Knossos papers are also deposited
there. Study of these not only vindicated Fyfe's accuracy but
the data he recorded in his measuring books has made it possible
to detect certain important architectural elements of the palace
which have been partly concealed by modern reconstructions.

The visitor in this vexed situation will demand frankness from
his guide. What he needs above all are hard facts. As we go round
the site I shall state at each key point what was found by the
excavator. For my knowledge I rely on the records, which include
unpublished photographs taken at the time of the excavation. I
shall quote Mackenzie's statements, Evans's own notebooks, the
papers of the architect Fyfe and the results of excavations by
Pendlebury. The statements made in the monumental work *The
Palace of Minos* have been checked in the first place against the

excavation reports published at the beginning of the century. Where there is discrepancy or doubt I have consulted the primary records. At the end of the tour of the palace the visitor will be apprised of the new picture which has emerged. In all simplicity it may be said that there was serious misreporting of the excavation. Indeed, not one of the key stratigraphical statements in Evans's *système de classification* has stood up to examination. The errors affect all periods: Early Minoan, Middle Minoan, Late Minoan.

The Palace

The palace we are approaching has a complex architectural history, all the more difficult to unravel because, with the exception of the East Wing, all that remained for the excavators to unearth were basement areas. The First Palace appears to have been built at the beginning of the Middle Minoan Period, which is now given an absolute date on the new low chronology of about 1700 B.C. It was a typical Cretan palace in that it was built around a Central Court which was about twice as long as it was broad (see Plan I). This palace was remodelled after an earthquake which Evans dated just before the close of the Middle Minoan Period, but the reconstructed building still retained its old lines. What occasioned the most baffling architectural complexities was the seizure of Knossos by the Mycenaean Greeks. These new occupiers introduced drastic changes to suit their own needs and tastes, particularly in the part of the palace which lies to the west of the Central Court. It is to this hybrid 'Last Palace', the remodelling of which took place at the earliest in the fourteenth century B.C. and possibly as late as the thirteenth century, that most of the famous works of 'Minoan' art discovered at Knossos belong. This period of the Palace and of Aegean art history deserves a special appellation. I propose to call it 'Late Creto-Mycenaean'.

1. The West Court

We approach the Palace from the Guard's House and enter the West Court. Originally a ramp led up to it, and this has now been provided with concrete steps. Before entering the Palace proper we can use the Court as a training ground to familiarize ourselves with archaeological methods and ways of thinking.

The West Court is paved with irregular flags, which may once have been covered with plaster. When was the pavement laid?

31

The Palace

The archaeologist seeks an answer to this question by probing below the pavement. In such test pits the fragments of pottery are collected and classified according to style. Evidently the pavement will be later than the latest type of sherds found underneath it. Evans did in fact make numerous probes below the pavement of the West Court. One of them, as reported by him, yielded a

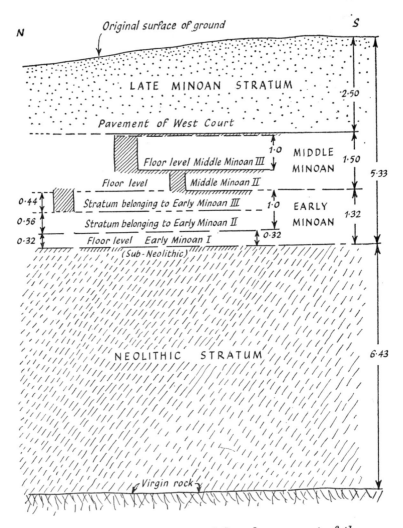

Fig. 1. Stratigraphic section below the pavement of the West Court (from the excavation report of 1904).

Plate I. The South Propylaeum area at the time of excavation looking south-west from the Central Court: (1) surviving pavement slabs in the south-west corner of the Central Court; (2) foundation blocks of the façade of the Last Palace; (3) north side of the 'megaron' foundations; (4) the 'altar base'; (5) north wall of the Room of the Clay Chest; (6) door-jambs of entrance to Room of the Chariot Tablets.

section of fundamental importance for Aegean archaeology. It revealed a succession of meticulously measured strata and floor levels, each characterized by its special type of pottery. The famous West Court Section (our Fig. 1), with its succession of Early Minoan, Middle Minoan and Late Minoan strata, formed the basis of Evans's *système de classification*, which he communicated to an international congress in Athens in the spring of 1905. In the autumn of that year, however, a letter from his excavator Mackenzie[12] apprised his employer of the true excavation data. He wrote: 'As regards an Early Minoan series, I cannot understand how you came to imagine such a series either from the West Square Section or anywhere else at Knossos'. He revealed to Evans the bald facts: the workmen had been left to themselves and they had missed the floor levels. The total amount of Early Minoan deposit found occupied about one cubic metre with no clear upper or lower limit. None of the scanty pottery was floor deposit and all of it was fragmentary. Evans had been absent from Knossos when the test pits had been dug and he had made his important scientific communication to the congress without having seen the evidence from his own excavation. The section he published was due to a misunderstanding of an 'ideal' section Mackenzie had drawn as a working hypothesis in his Day Book.

This first example illustrates the serious problems of reliability which Knossos presents to the modern investigator. Doro Levi, after recent excavations at Phaestos, came to the conclusion that the Early Minoan period, to which Evans had allotted close on a thousand years, was no more than a short transitional phase between Neolithic and Middle Minoan. Levi's results were apparently in conflict with those from the West Court Section at Knossos. Now, thanks to the discovery of Mackenzie's letter to Evans, we know that the test pits of 1904 necessitated little or no change in the statement made by Evans in the excavation report for 1903: 'There was no stratum here of that transitional Early Metal type to which the name Early Minoan has been applied'. Thus the results of Knossos agree with the recent results from Phaestos, and close on a thousand years of prehistory are eliminated. As for Middle Minoan, in agreement with the Swedish scholar Paul Åström, Levi would down-date it by some two hundred years. This would mean that the first Cretan palaces were built in the eighteenth century B.C. At this stage the writing system known as Linear A was already in use.

We can now pose our next archaeological question. What was the construction date of the 'Last Palace', the palace which housed the Linear B tablets and so many works of 'Minoan art'? This will be most effectively answered within the Palace itself, but in the West Court it means asking when the pavement was laid; and this again boils down to finding out what was the latest type of pottery underneath the pavement. The first probe below the paving slabs was made in 1901, and its position was entered on an unpublished plan by Fyfe which is preserved in the Ashmolean Museum. It was sunk at a point close to where we entered the West Court. There was a twofold stratification: 'Mycenaean' sherds lay above Middle Minoan. At that date 'Mycenaean' was used in rather a vague sense, but at least it did not mean Middle Minoan. In 1904 a different answer to the problem was obtained. Evans reported a stratum of Middle Minoan III B immediately below the pavement of the West Court (see Plan I for the find spot). This implied that the pavement in its latest form had been laid when MM III B pottery had already got stratified. Thus the evidence, as presented, indicated that the pavement was datable to the first Late Minoan period, or in round terms to the sixteenth century B.C. However, in 1930 renewed probing below the level of the Court pavement west of the Middle Minoan houses, yielded evidence which greatly mystified the excavator. To understand his bewilderment we must first locate the place of these excavations of 1930, when Pendlebury was his assistant.

It will be seen that slightly raised walks or 'causeways' lead through the Court east and north-east, the latter diagonal causeway joining up with another which runs north from the West Porch along the west façade of the Palace. Immediately to the left (i.e. north) of the diagonal causeway the visitor will see three circular walled pits (see Plan I). These 'koulouras', as they are called, were not visible at the time when the West Court was first cleared, since they underlay its surface. They had been filled up with masses of broken pottery to provide a foundation for the pavement. Such elaborate pits could hardly have been constructed originally to serve as rubbish pits, as has been suggested. It was just to the north of this line of ancient storage pits that Evans and Pendlebury made their surprising discoveries. To grasp their significance it is vital to know how far the surface had been cleared by previous excavation before they began their explorations below that surface. Fortunately there is photographic evidence from as early as 1901, and it is clear that the buildings and other structures uncovered in 1930 lay well below the surface of the West Court as determined by the surviving parts of the pavement, laid bare in 1900–1.

In 1930, the two westerly 'koulouras' were discovered. Then, a little further north, the excavator uncovered the lower walls of some houses which had been razed when the pavement of the West Court had been laid over their wall stumps. Again a photograph was taken,* and this shows the rooms deep below the surface. Many of these have been since covered up, but some can still be seen on the west side. It was in one of these rooms that Evans found a piece of pottery which puzzled him. It showed by way of decoration two swimming ducks in an environment of conventionalized papyri (Fig. 2a).

The reason for Evans's bewilderment was that this sherd was classified by him as Late Minoan III A, a style to which he gave an absolute date of the first quarter of the fourteenth century. This classification and date is accepted by modern authorities. But how could a vase datable to about 1375 B.C., that is some twenty-five years later than the supposed final destruction of the Palace, get deep below the surface of the West Court? The find circumstances were exactly like those of the Middle Minoan pots which were recovered just to the east in 1903–4, and had been used to justify the conclusion that the pavement was laid in the First Late Minoan period. Since a floor must be later than the latest sherds found below it, unless the plea of 'intrusion' is entered, the 'swimming ducks' sherd discovered in 1930 would invite the conclusion that the pavement was laid some time after 1375 B.C. But perhaps there was no occasion for surprise in 1930. The excavator had doubtless forgotten the test of 1901 on the other side of the

* An excellent reproduction was published in *The Palace of Minos* IV, 62, Fig. 36.

Fig. 2. (a) *Late Minoan III sherd (fourteenth century* B.C.) *found below the surface of the West Court in 1930;* (b) *bronze ewer from the North-west Treasure House;* (c) *sherds of 'Palace Style' from the West Palace borders;* (d) *Linear B tablet.*

diagonal causeway which had yielded 'Mycenaean' sherds below the pavement. It is a pity that the material from this test has disappeared. So for the time being the point may be put provisionally to a reserve account. Abundant evidence of the same stratigraphic pattern will appear within the Palace.

The complex basement spaces so surprisingly uncovered deep below the surface of the West Court thirty years after the beginning of the excavations contained another important find, this time of great interest not only for the chronology of the palace but also for Minoan religion. A large jar resting on the floor of one of the rooms contained a whole series of ritual vessels connected with snake worship. Evans immediately pointed out their close similarity to ritual furniture known previously from small domestic shrines discovered elsewhere in Crete. Now scholars are generally agreed that these shrines are late. In fact the finds from them (Gournia and Prinias) are exhibited in the Archaeological Museum in the room devoted to the 'Minoan Post-Palatial Period 1400–1100 B.C.' (see p. 125). At these sites the said ritual vessels are associated with rustic clay figures of goddesses, and the latter give us an important cross-reference. For such crude figures were also found in a shrine in the south-east quarter of the palace at Knossos which we shall visit late in the tour (see p. 104 on the Shrine of the Double Axes). There we shall have occasion to discuss the whole 'squatter' hypothesis and its bearing on Aegean history. But for the time being we may note that the experts are generally agreed both on the late date of this shrine and of the material to which Evans compared his finds from the 'Snake Room', unearthed so deep below the surface of the West Court. It reinforces the witness of the 'swimming ducks' sherd found in the same year.

It was in 1903 that yet another discovery in the West Court, this time in the northern part, suggested that the age of the imagined 'squatters' was in fact a period of high artistic production. One of the puzzling things to emerge from the Linear B tablets at Pylos was a number of references to bronze tripods 'of Cretan workmanship'. It would be natural to interpret such entries as reflecting relations with Crete. But at the time when the Pylos tablets were written (circa 1200 B.C.) Crete was supposed to have lapsed into poverty and isolation from the rest of the Aegean world for something like two centuries. What evidence have we from Crete itself of distinctively Cretan bronzework during the Late Minoan III period?

In the early excavation reports Evans had noted the dearth of bronze objects within the Palace, and he had attributed this poverty to the thoroughness with which the Palace had been sacked before its destruction. But in the fourth year's campaign he found what was called the Northwest Treasury (see Plan I). This structure, now covered up, stretched westwards in the northern part of the West Court. Throughout this complex building a regular stratification was observed. The top layer showed floors and pottery belonging to the Late Minoan III B period, that is the time of the hypothetical 'squatters'. Below these floors were others on which were found Late Minoan II pots ('Palace Style'). About a metre of deposit separated the two sets of floors. It was at the upper level that Evans made his exciting discovery of 1903 in the shape of a set of bronze vessels of exquisite workmanship (Fig. 2b). Mackenzie drew in his notebook the two different floors, each with its column base. The bronzes were found at a level corresponding to the upper floor level (Late Minoan III B). In *The Palace of Minos* Mackenzie's diagram[13] is reproduced, but the late upper floor with its column base has been omitted. Evans assigned the fine bronzes to the deeper lying Late Minoan II floor levels and he dated them accordingly. For him it was unthinkable to attribute such fine work to 'squatters'. But now that they are recognized as a myth invented by Evans we may take the excavation evidence at its face value. During the Late Minoan III B period the Northwest Treasury still stood in the north part of the West Court and it was involved in the final destruction of the Palace, perhaps as late as the twelfth century B.C.

The Northwest Treasury thus flanked the West Court on its north side. From this northern part of the Court we now make our way southwards along the west wall of the Palace towards the Southwest Portico. To our right, opposite Magazine XIII (see Plan I), a low rectangular structure can be seen, which the excavators interpreted as an altar base. Just beyond this altar the deposit alongside the west wall yielded important evidence often quoted in archaeological discussions about the history of the Palace. We are told that the Last Palace was a Late Minoan II palace. This implies that the bulk of the pottery found in the destruction debris was of Late Minoan II type, in other words the so-called Palace Style. The chief find place quoted for this type of pottery is the point where we are now standing, and the pieces occurred at a high level in the deposit on either side of the west wall. What is not generally realized is how meagre the finds were. The fragments nearly all belonged to a single vase and they were so few that the vase could only be restored because more complete vases showing a similar pattern were known from the Greek mainland. Our Fig. 2c reproduces the figure published by Mackenzie[14], which shows how small a part of the whole vase the actual sherds represented. The more complete Palace Style vases from 'the west Palace border', which are constantly reproduced in archaeological books and offered as evidence for dating the palace, were in fact obtained from earlier floor levels in the area of the Northwest Treasure House. They were not recovered from the destruction debris of the palace itself. Apart from this, the main source of 'Palace Style' ware from Knossos presented by Evans was a rubbish pit between the South Terrace of the Palace and the South House (see below). So much for the 'Late Minoan II Palace'.

If we now make the necessary corrections to Evans's published West Court Section in the light of the new knowledge obtained from his records, a curious and puzzling pattern presents itself as regards the Late Minoan Period. In the Northwest Treasure House all is well. There, Late Minoan III A–B is stratified about one metre above Late Minoan II. But how are we to explain the fragments of Late Minoan II high in the deposit above the pavement? This is a stratigraphical inversion. The answer is simple, as we shall see when we visit the 'Magazines' on the other side of the West Wall. A deep hole had been dug in one of them (Magazine VIII) by the Turkish proprietor before Evans purchased the site. He had even broken through the pavement and penetrated into the underlying chests. These new fragments of LM II pottery close to the surface belonged to the top part of the upcast, which naturally came from the deepest part of the pit which had been dug. Thus if we restore them to their proper place, we have the same stratification on both sides of the West Wall. The point will be taken up again once we have reached that part of the palace interior (see p. 59).

The massive wall which forms the West Façade of the palace is of complex construction. It has a projecting plinth of limestone, which is a levelling course ('euthunteria'). On this rests another course of massive dressed blocks of gypsum (the orthostates or 'standers'). The wall is some six feet thick, and its interior east face is also finished with orthostates the same height as those on the exterior. Strength and elasticity were given to the whole construction by crossbars of wood dovetailed into the upper surfaces of the stone blocks. The space between the two facings was filled with a rubble core. This core was found to contain sherds as late as Late Minoan III.

The West Façade does not run in a straight line, but projects and recedes, so that the magazines which it encloses form blocks of different length. Roughly in the middle of each section there are shallow recesses (see Plan I), which have been taken as indications of window recesses at the upper floor level. Smoke stains are still visible on the gypsum orthostates of the West Wall. From the traces Evans deduced that when the final conflagration was blazing a strong wind had been blowing from the south. This wind is common in the spring in Crete.

The exterior wall, for all its massiveness, had no deep foundations but rests on a bedding of small irregular stones. This has been taken as indicating that the upper storeys of the Palace were in all probability of light construction, being built of sun-dried brick strengthened with a wooden framework. The height of the magazines and service rooms on the ground floor and in the basements has been calculated as from 9–10 feet, while the living and reception rooms were 12–14 feet. According to one estimate, the total height of the façade at Knossos is not likely to have exceeded 40–45 feet. The roof was probably flat, with perhaps a slight slope for drainage. This has been deduced from the absence of roof tiles in the ruins and the shape of the ground plan.

The Palace

2. THE SOUTH PROPYLAEUM AREA

We now proceed towards the West Porch, which lies at the south-east corner of the West Court. A little beyond the point where the west façade makes its deep return east a line of large slabs can be seen in the pavement to the east of the raised causeway. At the south end the line curves away to the east towards the west wall. These slabs are part of the foundations of the West Wall of the First Palace, when there was an entrance facing west approached by the west-east causeway. The Last Palace had its west façade set back, and a new entrance system was devised running north-south. The West Porch, which we are about to enter, was the ceremonial entrance to this palace, as is apparent from the convergence of the raised causeways. The porch has a single column, and there is evidence that it is a later addition to the architecture of the Entrance Lodge. First there is the asymmetrical placing of the column. More important is the fact that the projecting plinth of the West Wall has been cut away from a point where the front line of the porch would have intersected it. From this the excavators concluded that what had once been outside wall was made into interior wall by the building of the porch. The now awkward section of the plinth was hacked away and the wall of the porch was plastered over and decorated with scenes representing bull fighting above a dado painted with squares imitating marble. As we shall see, a bull scene also greeted visitors to the palace who used the Northern Entrance Passage. The 'Palace of Minos' may justly also be called 'The Palace of the Bull'.

The porch gives access to a kind of porter's lodge, comprising a larger outer room with a smaller inner room to the west, which may have served as a bedroom. The arrangement now on view is a restoration of an earlier phase of the palace. In the last stage of occupation, as excavated in 1900, the large room had been much reduced in size by the construction of poorly built walls that are marked in broken lines on Plan I. Theodore Fyfe, on an unpublished plan of the palace preserved in Oxford, marked these walls as belonging to the Late Mycenaean Period. They can also be seen on a photograph of the porch taken in 1900. Once these walls had been built there was no longer any access to the inner room, which had evidently passed out of use.

The late date of the final remodelling of the West Porch was further indicated by a piece of evidence secured during supplementary excavations in 1905. Parts of the adjacent pavement were lifted in the hope of finding clues bearing on the construction date of the last palatial phase. One find was of particular interest to Evans in view of his long-standing concern with seal stones. One of these objects was found alongside the threshold of the West Porch below the level of the pavement. In technique and style it was immediately diagnosed by Evans as characteristic of the Late Minoan II period. The find position would normally have indicated that the threshold had been laid after this seal stone had found its way into the ground. But by 1905 Evans's ideas about the history of the palace had solidified, and he dismissed this piece of evidence by stating that it had 'worked down beside the threshold'.[15] As we shall see, the threshold of the Throne Room suite likewise sealed in late material (see below p. 67).

From the inner room looking west we can see below us a complex building which was constructed only after the massive palace foundations running east-west had been cut into and removed. We shall visit this intrusive building at the end of the tour. In his *Guide*, Pendlebury, following Evans, attributes this building to a powerful noble who had encroached on the palace during the Middle Minoan III Period. As we shall see, in fact it belongs to the Late Minoan III Period like the latest alteration to the porch itself, and it gives us some idea of the elaborate building work carried out in the so-called 'squatter' period.

It was 'near the south-west entrance', as Evans recorded in his 1900 notebook, that an important Linear B tablet was found. It records at least 1800 stirrup-jars. It was this fact which first raised doubts about the published version of the last phase of the Palace. For Evans repeatedly insisted that not a single stirrup-jar belonging to this phase had been found in the ruins, although this type of vessel was extremely common during the post-palatial Late Minoan III period. The distinction is also made in the *système de classification*. How, then, could the inhabitants of the Late Minoan II Palace be recording such great quantities of a type of vessel which did not come into common use until the following post-palatial period? It remains to add that Evans transferred this particular tablet to the northwest part of the palace and incorporated it in his 'decisive stratigraphy', which was offered as a proof of the earlier date of the tablets.

From the West Porch we enter the Corridor of the Procession, which was also decorated with frescoes. The fragments have been reconstructed (see below, p. 126) as a procession of youths and girls bringing offerings to a goddess. This corridor originally continued south before turning left (east) along the front of the palace to reach the South Propylaeum. The south-west angle of the palace, however, has collapsed down the slope, where the massive blocks of the retaining wall can be seen scattered. So we have to turn left from the corridor (following the arrows on Plan I) and right again through a narrow door (see Plan I, 1). This is the door referred to by Evans in his early notes as 'the southwest door'. It is of considerable archaeological interest because right at the start of the excavation in 1900 a tablet was found here containing a man's name which recurs on another tablet found in the East Wing in the following season. It has recently been shown that the two tablets were written by the same scribe, so that there can be no doubt that the two tablets are contemporary products. Thus we have a valuable archaeological cross-reference between the west and east wings of the palace.

From the Southwest Door we look down towards the outside building known as the South House. It was in the space between this house and the south terrace wall of the palace (Plan I, 2) that the greatest quantity of the pottery known as Late Minoan II was found. This figures largely in chronological discussions of the palace. It cannot be regarded, however, as belonging to the Last Palace, because Mackenzie records it as having been thrown out as rubbish during repairs to the palace in the Third Late Minoan Period. This means that the pottery in question is evidence for the penultimate phase. Evans classified them as Late Minoan II. Later, the sherds were studied by the Swedish expert A. Furumark and he classified many of them as Late Minoan III A. Thus we again have evidence supporting that from the West Court: the Last Palace, i.e. the Creto-Mycenaean building, was constructed, or at least re-modelled, when Late Minoan III A pottery had already been discarded.

After passing through the Southwest Door we turn left and reach the South Propylaeum,[16] which is entered by a triple doorway. It was at this point that the excavations began in 1900. The earth covering was less than a metre deep. Almost immediately intact jars were uncovered with their rims a few centimetres below the grass (Plan II, 1). One of these has been placed on the terminal part of a spur of wall on the left, which at the time of the excavation projected from the west wall of the Propylaeum (Plan I, 3). On this west wall, now reconstructed to full height, a replica of the Cupbearer Fresco has been mounted, the fragments of which were found in the corridor to the west (see Plan II).

This is the part of the site which presents the greatest difficulty both for guide and visitor, for there has been wholesale reconstruction and removal of what was actually found by the excavators. In front of us we see a monumental staircase (Plan I, 5) leading up to the first storey which is known as the Piano Nobile. All this must be thought away if we are to form some conception of what the Last Palace, that is the Creto-Mycenaean Palace, was like. Evans has almost completely removed an important later structure and used the materials to build his imaginary staircase.

The part of the site occupied by this staircase at the time of the excavation was virtually an archaeological blank which in the first reports was called the Central Clay Area, because of the deposit of virgin clay. It was not until 1907 that it was discovered that the clay was the bedding of a rectangular building, the foundations of which (marked on Plan II) went deep down below the surface of the clay. The massive limestone blocks comprising these foundations have now been largely removed and used to construct the bastions of the staircase. Fortunately, a photograph was taken at the time of the excavation (Plate I), and comparison with the modern photograph (Plate II) will enable the visitor to judge the transformation effected by the restorer. The photograph of Plate I was taken from point 6 of Plan I. Plan II should be consulted along with this Plate. We first go into the Central Court to take our bearings.

We look north towards the Northern Entrance Passage, which

will be visited later in the tour. On the east side of the Court to our right lies the Domestic Quarter; on our left is the West Wing, which is divided into two by the Long Corridor of the Magazines running south-north. The block which lies to the east of this corridor and faces the Central Court is divided by a flight of steps leading up from the Central Court to the upper floor. To the north of the steps lies the Throne Room block, while to the south is the suite of rooms centring on the Lobby of the Stone Seat outside which (Plan I, 6), the photograph Plate I was taken. Standing at this point we look south-west. Plate I shows the scene in 1900 looking towards the rectangular space where the flight of steps has been built. On the left of the photograph can be seen the surviving group of limestone paving slabs in the south-west corner of the Central Court (Plate I, 1). Coming towards us is the line of the foundation blocks of the palace façade (Plate I, 2). About the middle of the photograph the sharp edge of a line of masonry can be seen. This is the foundation wall of the rectangular building (Plate I, 3), forming the north boundary of the Central Clay Area.

This massive course of masonry is one clue to the puzzle we have to solve: what was the shape and form of the Creto-Mycenaean Palace occupied by the dynasts of Knossos? In the present case the question takes the specific form: was the rectangular building part of the Linear B Palace? In the deposit with much carbon ash an important hoard of tablets was found heaped up close to the north face of the rectangular building (Plate I, 3); but the facts have been obscured by the later reconstructions which involved the total removal of the wall. Thus we must proceed step by step to restore the original position.

In the foreground of Plate I a flight of steps can be seen leading down to the pavement of the Lobby of the Stone Seat.[17] A collapsed jar is visible against the wall, and to the right of this is a pair of stone door-jambs. We descend the steps and pass through this doorway, which leads to a little room (Plan II, 9). At the time of the excavation the back wall of the room was formed by the said foundation wall of the rectangular 'megaron', and the room was divided into two by a low bench jutting out from the east wall (Plan II, 8). It was in the narrow space between the bench and the back wall that one of the richest hoards of Linear B tablets was found. They are of particular interest because many of them showed the outline of a chariot and a horse's head, and they give us some idea of the military equipment of the Mycenaean kings of Knossos. This room is consequently known as the Room of the Chariot Tablets.[18]

The tablets were discovered in 1900 in the first few weeks of the excavation. In 1909 Evans, after nine years of reflection on the evidence, published his considered conclusion that the Chariot Tablets had in all probability been stored in boxes placed on shelves attached to the back wall of the room, that is the north wall of the 'megaron'. This made it evident that the 'megaron' must have been an integral part of the Creto-Mycenaean Palace. The find facts which suggested this conclusion were these: the tablets were found mostly between the bench and the back wall in a deposit of carbon ash which extended from the floor to a height greater than the surviving courses of the wall. Along with the tablets were found clay sealings some of which showed traces of the cord with which the boxes containing the tablets had been fastened. There were also bronze hinges belonging to the boxes. The shelves attached to the wall and the wooden boxes themselves had been consumed in the great fire which put an end to the Creto-Mycenaean Palace — hence the plentiful carbon ash in which the tablets had been found.

The find facts utilized by Evans in 1909 are accurately represented in Plan II. But what the visitor now sees is wholly different. It represents what the excavator had come to believe when he wrote *The Palace of Minos* (1921–35). The 'megaron' foundations have been removed and the material used to build the open steps going up from the South Propylaeum. But one of the great limestone blocks has been left as a sample; it can be seen propped up against the wall at the foot of the staircase on the east side of the room. These stairs are also modern. In *The Palace of Minos*, contrary to the account of 1909, it is stated that the tablets were found in a cupboard below this staircase. Gone, too, is the low bench, except for the end part. The rest has been incorporated as ancient material in the reconstructed steps (see below). The present south wall of the Room of the Chariot Tablets is also modern.

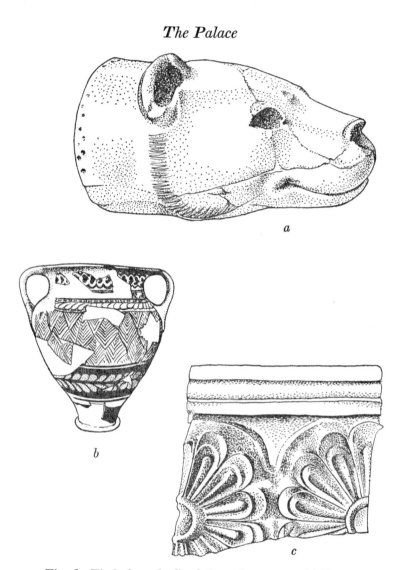

Fig. 3. Finds from the South Propylaeum area: (a) *lioness head rhyton;* (b) *reconstructed vase from inside the wall of the South Propylaeum;* (c) *carved stone rosettes.*

In this part of the site some famous works of 'Minoan art' were recovered. To the west of the Room of the Chariot Tablets lies a square chamber (Plan II, 10) where a fine set of stone ritual vessels was found. They included the remarkable Lioness Head Rhyton

The Palace

(Fig. 3a; see also below p. 122). The scatter of stone vessels, which had evidently fallen into these basement spaces from above, extended farther south, and a stone lamp was actually found within the area of the rectangular 'megaron' (Plan III 2).[19] Like the tablets, these stone vessels belonged to the Creto-Mycenaean Palace.

That the 'megaron' was an integral part of the Linear B Palace was confirmed by yet another find of tablets on the south side. To reach the find spot we ascend the steps which lead southwards from the Room of the Chariot Tablets and find ourselves in a room which is labelled 'The Temple of Rhea'. This is wholly fanciful. To sort things out we may begin with the rectangular block of slabs which occupies the centre of the room. The edge of this can be seen in Plate I, 4. At first the excavator believed it to be an altar base, and he called this space the Court of the Altar. Later it became clear that the 'altar base' was in fact the surviving ornamental centre of a room belonging to a palatial phase preceding the construction of the 'megaron'.

Further evidence of this earlier phase can be seen in Plate I. Just beyond the 'megaron' wall (Plate I, 3) and in front of the altar base a stone door-jamb can be seen projecting above the surface. It was one of four pairs, and from this four-fold doorway steps had once led down northwards to the basement areas centring on the Lobby of the Stone Seat. But these steps were blocked by the construction of the rectangular building (for details see Plan II) in the Mycenaean Period. Why, then, the 'Temple of Rhea'? Although Evans first regarded the 'megaron' as a Bronze Age building, he later came to believe that it was a Greek temple of the classical period; and he ascribed it to the goddess Rhea, who in Homer is the mother of the gods and of Zeus in particular. Thus the modern reconstruction has incorporated a feature of the penultimate 'Minoan' palace (the ornamental centre) into what purports to be a Greek temple of post-Mycenaean times. But what of the large hoard of Linear B tablets found in a carbon ash deposit heaped up against the foundation wall of a Greek temple? It was doubtless this difficulty which occasioned the displacement of the Chariot Tablets in the later account (*The Palace of Minos*) to a cupboard under stairs built for the purpose.

Plate II. View of the South Propylaeum area as reconstructed.

The Palace

From the 'Temple of Rhea' we pass southwards through a doorway and find ourselves in a little bathroom with a drain running underneath it. The remains of the bath tub are preserved *in situ* against the south wall. This room is again of great historical importance, because it provided the first considerable and coherent find of Linear B tablets made by the excavator. They were found, in a deposit of carbon ash, packed in rows in the bath tub. The excavator rightly concluded that a box must have fallen from the upper floor as a consequence of the fire which destroyed the Linear B Palace. What we have to do is to determine the relation of the bathroom to the rectangular 'megaron' to which it forms an annexe on the south side. This key question has been the subject of keen dispute. We can hardly doubt that the bathroom must have been built before the bath tub was put into it. In view of its content of tablets it is thus of vital importance to establish the position of the bathroom walls with respect to the foundations of the 'megaron'. Evidently, if the walls overlay the foundations, then the 'megaron' cannot be *later* than the bathroom. The early plans drawn by Evans's architect Fyfe show the bathroom walls running across the south foundation of the 'megaron'. Some doubts have been expressed about the accuracy of these plans. However, the recent discovery of Fyfe's measuring books, as well as a plan of the area drawn by Evans himself, has put the facts beyond dispute. The position of the north wall of the bathroom is given by Evans himself as 1·82 m south of the south side of the 'altar base'. This agrees with the published plans as well as with an important unpublished plan by T. Fyfe. The flimsy wall in question can be seen in the photograph (Plate I, 5) rising high above the surface of the 'altar base'. If we still wished to uphold Evans's theory that the rectangular building was later than the bathroom, the only course open to us would be to claim that the foundations of the 'megaron' lay *above* the bathroom walls. This has, in fact, been argued.* Once again Fyfe's measuring

---

* Note also that since the excavators cleared away the debris down to the Bronze Age floor level as represented by the base of the bath in 1900, this would have left the massive foundations of a 'Greek temple' suspended in mid air. This remarkable archaeological levitation passed unnoticed by visitors and excavators for seven years. It was not until 1907 that the existence of the rectangular foundations was reported (see Evans's communication to *The Times* 15 July 1907).

books settle the matter: they give the level of the foundation wall as 7 cm *below* the surface of the 'altar base'. Still better, the precise information in these books has enabled us to detect a piece of original evidence left untouched by the modern restorations. It was long believed that Evans had entirely removed the massive limestone blocks of the 'megaron' foundation and had used them to build the imposing flight of steps leading up to the 'Piano Nobile'. It turns out, however, that at least two of them have been left in position. It will be seen that the modern restored doorjambs of the doorway by which we entered the bathroom rest on a block of limestone which rises a little higher than the present floor of the bathroom. This block, in position, level, and dimensions, corresponds to Fyfe's notes and plans. Another such block can be seen on the other side of the present west wall of the bathroom. The case is proved: the bathroom was an integral part of the Creto-Mycenaean Palace, and the 'megaron' to which it was an annexe was not a later construction (a Greek temple) but a Bronze Age building, as Evans first reported.

The tablets found in the tub record a series of offerings to a number of divinities. By a curious chance, the tablet with which Evans began his Handlist of the tablets, started with the following entries: 'To the Daidaleion' (i.e. the shrine of Daedalus). . . .', For Dictaean Zeus. . . .'. If he had been able to read the tablets, as we now can, Evans would have known in the first week of the excavation that his palace had been occupied by Mycenaean Greeks, and he would not have been surprised at the presence of one of their typical rectangular halls.

The west wall of the bathroom is again a modern construction which replaces an original flimsy partition wall dividing the bathroom into two (see Plan II). In the inner compartment was found a bronze statuette which Evans in *The Palace of Minos* displaced and assigned to the Middle Minoan period. Alongside the bath tub a jar was found standing.[20] At Pylos, too, jars were found in the little bathroom, and there is little doubt that they must have contained water for the bather.

We now return to the Propylaeum to ask some key archaeological questions. When was it last occupied? The date is given by the groups of jars found here *in situ*. Many of them have been left on view, largely intact; they are classified as Late Minoan III B. But when was the Propylaeum constructed? Evidence bearing on the date is sought by looking for sherds incorporated in the masonry of the walls. In 1902 the spur of wall on the west side was partially demolished, only the end piece being left, that on which one of the jars now stands. Sherds were found inside the masonry and they were deposited in the Stratigraphical Museum at Knossos. Recently a vase has been reconstructed embodying the sherds, and it is now exhibited in the Archaeological Museum at Herakleion (see below p. 123 and Fig. 3b). It belongs to the Late Minoan III A type. Later excavations along the foundations of the west wall produced similar results but they went unreported. Again, in 1925 corroboratory evidence was found under the east wall. It was discovered that this wall had been built over an earlier sunken chest (see Plan II, 13), which had been filled in with debris to afford a firm footing for the wall. On the east side of the wall the fill of the chest contained sherds as late as Late Minoan III. Then a shaft was sunk on the west side of the chest and a tunnel was made underneath it.[21] Again Late Minoan III was obtained. Thus the South Propylaeum, like the rectangular 'megaron', was actually constructed in the Late Minoan III Period. It represented a drastic remodelling of the Minoan palace by the Greek intruders. Evans himself commented on the masonry: he said in effect that it is the ruin of a ruin and looks like the work of the 'Decadence'. These intruders, as we now know, were Mycenaean Greeks, who inserted into the 'Minoan Palace' a rectangular mainland 'megaron' with a bathroom and other service rooms to the south. To this Creto-Mycenaean phase belong not only the tablets in the room which flank the 'megaron' on its north and south sides, but also the frescoes, the bronze statuette and the magnificent set of ritual vessels, including the Lioness Head Rhyton.

One find from this area was repeatedly used by Evans in his dispute with Wace over the date of the 'beehive' tombs at Mycenae. Evans was concerned to prove that Wace's date, the thirteenth century B.C., was far too late. In fact Evans believed that the constructions were erected in Middle Minoan III A times, that is in absolute terms in the early seventeenth century B.C. To support this contention he produced as evidence some finely carved pieces of stone (see Fig. 3c), which showed a remarkable stylistic resemblance to those from the façade of the Treasury of Atreus at Mycenae. The similarity of design and technique was such that Evans held that they must have emanated from the same school of stone carving if not from one and the same craftsman. That they were contemporary products he did not doubt. To demolish Wace's date Evans alleged a clear stratification of the Knossos find: it was unearthed 70 cm below the Middle Minoan III B floor in the South Propylaeum, and this evidently indicated a Middle Minoan III A date. It is now clear, thanks to a plan drawn by Evans in his 1900 notebook, that the piece of carved stone was found at point 15 of Plan II, that is between the two groups of LM III B pithoi, some 20 cm *above* their bases and 70 cm below the surface before excavation. Thus the true find facts, revealed by Evans's own notebook, support Wace's late date for the construction of the Treasury of Atreus. The stylistic resemblance so strongly insisted on by Evans may now be turned against him: it is evidence for the LM III date of the architectural decoration of the Last Palace at Knossos.

We now ascend the flight of stone steps leading to the 'Piano Nobile', from which a fine view can be obtained looking south towards Mount Juktas — a favourite theme of photographers. Here note the pieces of original stone incorporated in the steps. These were taken from the low bench in the Room of the Chariot Tablets (see above). The whole of the upper floor is imaginary and none of the ancient elements incorporated here and there to give it verisimilitude was actually found there. In preparation for the next stage of the tour, the visitor should go to the west side of the Piano Nobile and look down on the West Magazines, with their rows of large storage jars and sunken receptacles along the middle of the floor. Magazines VIII–XII have been built over, but the buttress which can be seen built into a chest in the middle of Magazine VII is of particular architectural interest and importance. It is matched by another built into Magazine IX, and they both supported columns in an upper hall (see later and cf. Plan I).

We now descend to the Central Court and return to the Lobby of the Stone Seat, so-called from the bench against its north

a

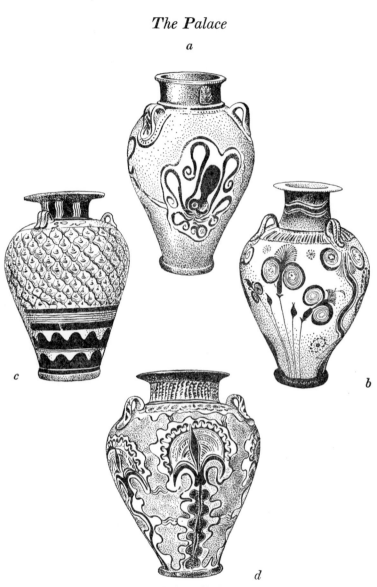

c

b

d

Fig. 4. 'Palace Style' pottery.

wall. Some of the rooms opening off it have shallow rectangular basins sunk into the floor, and alongside them stood storage jars. From this Evans concluded that the rooms had been used for the storage of liquids, probably oil. This was proved to be correct by a set of tablets found just to the east of the stone bench, which

Fig. 5. Faience figures from the Temple Repositories:
(a) the Snake Goddess; (b) a votary.

itself was flanked by a large jar, the remnants of which can still be seen. The texts record the issue of olive oil to a variety of recipients. We may suppose that the officials controlling the issue of the stock of oil kept in this set of rooms sat on the stone bench in the lobby and recorded their outgoings and incomings.

The construction of the rubble walls here is particularly to be noted, as also are the marks of fire. The door at the north-west corner leads to a little room (Plan I, 7) called the Room of the Tall Pithos, after the giant jar which still stands there. However, other jars 'of the usual late character' (Evans) were also found, while a stirrup-jar, the standard oil container of the Mycenaeans, lay on its side in the doorway.

The next room to the north (Plan I, 8) is of exceptional interest. Here two architectural phases can be seen. During the time of the Last Palace the floor had the same sunken shallow basins as in the Room of the Tall Pithos, but later excavation showed that the shallow receptacles had been constructed over earlier chests which had been much larger and deeper. The lower chests were found to contain remarkable treasures of a ritual character, including the famous faience figure of a Snake Goddess and her votaries (Fig. 5), to say nothing of a Linear A tablet. Thus we have in this part of the palace evidence for two archaeological periods, each with its associated script, Linear A and Linear B. The Linear A tablet from the lower chest records large quantities of some kind of liquid, which was possibly linseed oil.

We now pass through the doorway on the west side of the Lobby of the Stone Seat and enter the East Pillar Room (Plan I, 9) with its massive pillar incised with the signs of the double axe. Evans thought that this was a pillar shrine, but the same kind of jars were found here as in the other rooms, as well as the shallow basins. This indicates that at least in the last phase of the palace this room was also used for the storage of oil. We pass into the West Pillar Room (Plan I, 10) and turn left along a corridor flanked by long narrow storage rooms. This corridor was called by Evans the Corridor of the House Tablets. He thought that the ideogram on the tablets found here represented a house; but it is now known that the sign in question stands for aromatic substances, including coriander.

The Palace

3. THE WEST MAGAZINES[22]

At the end of the Corridor of the House Tablets we turn right and emerge into the Long Corridor of the Magazines, which gives access to a series of long, narrow store-rooms opening off it on the west side. This corridor was cleared in 1900, and a photograph taken at the time (Plate III) gives us important archaeological information. Evans described the corridor in the first excavation report as one of the most striking sights in the whole building: 53 metres long with a 'finely compacted pavement' of gypsum slabs. In the photograph a cross wall can be seen at the north end beyond the flight of steps. The purpose of this barrier, which was a later addition, was to shut off the northern group of magazines from the Long Corridor. These magazines (numbers XIV–XVIII), had a different function from the southern group. The latter were lined with rows of large jars, and most of them, as we saw, had the shallow stone-lined receptacles ('cists') sunk into the floor. Evans saw that these magazines were evidently intended for the storage

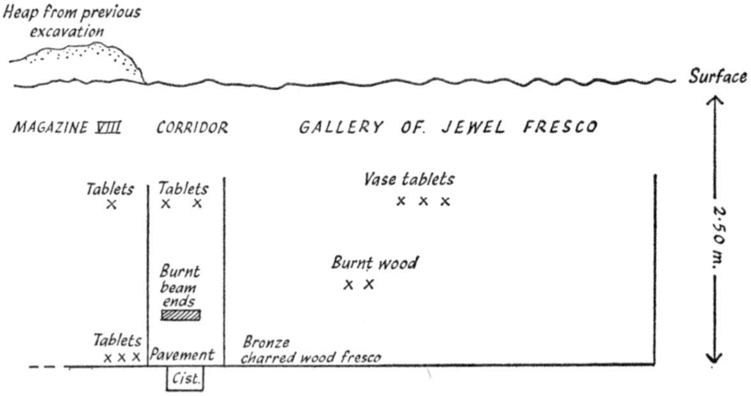

Fig. 6. Stratigraphic section in the area of the Vase Tablets. The Gallery of the Jewel Fresco contained the LM III B strainer assigned by Evans to the Room of the Stirrup-Jars. The pavement of the Long Corridor, found complete in 1900, was lifted in 1903. The cists of a former phase which underlay it contained LM III A and B pottery, some of it showing marks of conflagration.

of liquids. The northern magazines had no jars and no cists, while the floors were of cement and not of gypsum slabs. From the tablets found in the northern group, especially in Magazine XV, it would appear that they were used for the storage of textiles.

At a point opposite Magazine VIII (Plan I, 11) Evans found an instructive pattern of archaeological facts which is summarized in Fig. 6. The remnants of burnt ceiling beams from the final conflagration had subsided to about 16–20 inches above the pavement of the corridor. Still higher, close to the surface, Linear B tablets had been scattered from a magazine on the east side of the corridor (Magazine of the Vase Tablets, see Plan I) into Magazine VIII. It was evident that there had been no disturbance to the deposit since the great fire destroyed the Creto-Mycenaean Palace. In the fourth year of the excavations, that is in 1903, Evans lifted the paving slabs of the corridor and recorded his surprise at discovering that the closely compacted pavement had been laid over cists belonging to a former architectural phase of the palace. These cists ran the whole length of the corridor from opposite Magazine IV to opposite Magazine XIII. When the Last Palace was constructed, the cists had been filled in with miscellaneous debris, and the fill had then been covered with a layer of clay to act as a bedding for the paving slabs.

Here was a classical 'closed deposit' to which archaeologists rightly attach decisive importance. Evidently, the latest sherds in the fill underneath the pavement and its clay bedding must be earlier than the pavement. The sherds obtained in the 1903 exploration of the cists are housed in the Stratigraphical Museum at Knossos. The material has recently been re-examined. Much of it is Late Minoan III and it includes not merely sherds but whole pots of this late date. What is of especial interest is that some of the material shows marks of burning.[23] As the visitor stands on the pavement opposite Magazine VIII he may ponder the pattern of finds in the Long Corridor at this point (see the section Fig. 6).[24] About the level of his knees the burnt ceiling beams were found. Above his head was the scatter of tablets extending into Magazine VIII. Below the pavement on which he stands the fill of the disused cists contained burnt Late Minoan III material. The conclusion seems inescapable: the Last Palace, the Creto-

Mycenaean Palace with its Linear B tablets, was constructed after
a fire which had involved Late Minoan III pottery. In other words,
the result was the same as that obtained in the West Court and
the South Propylaeum: the Penultimate Palace was destroyed not
earlier than the fourteenth century B.C. and possibly as late as the
thirteenth century B.C.

The results of the 1903 test excavations in the Long Corridor
were repeated when Evans re-examined Magazine XIII in 1904.
Here, too, we have valuable records in the shape of photographs.
As first excavated in 1901, this magazine had a row of the usual
shallow oil cists running along the middle of the pavement. These
were completely cleared of deposit in the excavations of that year.
A photograph taken at the time (see Plate IV) shows these cists
still intact. Three years later, that is in 1904, Evans, with the
declared purpose of securing evidence bearing on the early history
of the palace, lifted the bottom slabs of the cists to see what was
underneath. Once again it turned out that the shallow cists had
been reconstructed by remodelling earlier cists which had been
much deeper. The latter are what the visitor sees today, and he
should compare Plate IV, which shows what they looked like
during the period of the Last Palace. The earlier cists had first
been filled in with miscellaneous debris and the bottom slabs of
the remodelled cists were placed above it. The sherds which were
obtained from the fill of the lower cists are preserved in the
Stratigraphical Museum. This material, too, has been recently
examined and it is reported that all the boxes contain Late Minoan
III sherds, some of them showing marks of burning.[25] This
corroborates the findings of 1903 below the pavement of the Long
Corridor and imposes the same conclusion. The Last Palace must
be later than the burnt Late Minoan III pottery found in the
debris below its floors. The final occupation of the Palace is
represented by the pots seen in the photograph on Plate IV and
by the Linear B tablets found in the conflagration debris.

The general lay-out of the magazines may now be considered
(see Plan I). It will be seen that they form three blocks: III–V,
VI–X, XI–XVI, the outer walls of these blocks being distinctly
thicker than the partition walls dividing the magazines within the
blocks. Especially noteworthy are the buttresses built against the

north wall of Magazine VII and the south wall of Magazine IX. These buttresses must be later than the cists, for they are built into them and over them. The lower part of the cists had first been filled in with compact masses of foundation blocks and then the piers were built up of small blocks of limestone. The southern half of the cist in Magazine VII was then paved over, the slabs being fitted to the outline of the buttress. This is clear in a photograph taken at the time.[26]

Once again we have an instructive pattern of archaeological facts. Evidently, any pottery found below this pavement must be earlier than it. Evans himself stated that part of a vase of 'Late Palace style' (that is Late Minoan II) was found between the buttress and the wall of the cist into which it had been built. This fact has significance for the whole structure of this wing of the Last Palace. For what purposes were these buttresses built? Evans saw that their function was to support the pillars of a hall in the storey above the magazines. Evidently this whole structure must be later than the Late Minoan II sherd below the pavement. It is a terminus post quem for the building of the buttress and the laying of the latest pavement of the magazine, to say nothing of the upper storey supported by the buttresses. If we now add the evidence of the Long Corridor and Magazine XIII and note further that LM II–III sherds were found in the rubble core of the West Wall, it will be clear that the whole west wing of the Last Palace was constructed when LM II–III pottery had already been used and discarded. The same absolute date emerges: the Last Palace was constructed not earlier than the fourteenth century B.C., and it was built over the ruins of a palace destroyed by fire.

Here in the magazines we may revert to the archaeological puzzle briefly mentioned while we were still in the West Court. Evans stressed from first to last that the chief find of 'Palace Style' pottery, which he used to date the Last Palace, was made in the West Magazines, at a high level, principally in Magazines VIII–X, with an overspill across the great West Wall at this point into the West Court. How can we explain this stratigraphical inversion: LM II at a high level in the debris, but LM III stratified below the pavement at so many points in the West Wing? Evans himself provided the answer.[27] He stated that before he came to

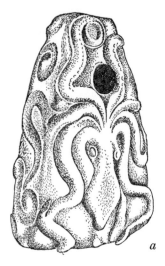

a

b

Fig. 7. Finds in the northern group of magazines: (a)
octopus weight; (b) carved stone decoration; (c) (opposite)
the 'Parisienne' fresco.

c

Knossos to start his excavations the native Mohametan proprietor
had dug a deep hole in Magazine VIII and had even penetrated
through the pavement exposing the underlying cists of the previous
palatial phase. Naturally, the upcast from the deepest part of the
hole would have been thrown up last. In this simple way the
observed stratigraphical 'inversion' was produced. We may
remind ourselves that the 'Palace Style' sherds obtained nearly
all belonged to a single vase (Fig. 2c) and this was so fragmentary
that it could only be restored on the model of more complete
specimens which had previously been found on the Greek mainland. This was the sum total of the evidence from within the

Palace offered by Evans for his Late Minoan II palace, apart from the sherds recovered from a rubbish dump between the South Terrace and the South House. The more complete Palace Style vases from 'the West Palace borders' which are so often reproduced in archaeological and popular works actually came from rooms below the surface of the West Court which had Late Minoan III floors above them.

Evidence for the decorative details of this part of the Palace points to the same chronological conclusion. To view the find spot we walk north along the corridor. After Magazine XIII it will be seen that there is no direct access to the magazines from the corridor until we come to Magazine XVII (see Plate IV and Plan I). At the time of the first excavation in 1900 a cross wall (Plan I, 12 and Plate III) blocked the corridor. Beyond this a doorway immediately on the left leads from Magazine XVII to XVI, and another at the west end of the south wall of this latter magazine opens into Magazine XV. At this point (Plan I, 13) a coherent hoard of tablets was found close to the surface. They listed pieces of finished cloth, apparently done up in bundles of five. Other tablets found hereabouts show that both men and women were concerned with the production of cloth, the men working in couples and the women in threes. Children of both sexes are listed with the women and it appears that some of these were 'in school', that is they were learning the crafts of textile manufacture. In Magazine XV was also found a weight of purple gypsum, its surfaces carved with octopuses in relief (Fig. 7a). The associations suggest that this weight was used to weigh wool and cloth. This 'great wool stone', if we may so call it, had much the same weight as the Babylonian talent (29 kilograms).

Behind Magazine XV is a space leading to Magazine XIV. Here were found the pieces of carved stone (Fig. 7b) which Evans compared to the very similar reliefs from Tiryns and Mycenae, and this indicates a thirteenth-century date for the Palace of Knossos. Associated with these was the famous piece of painted stucco 'La Parisienne' showing the bust of a girl with very large eyes and vermilion lips (Fig. 7c) — again a work of the Creto-Mycenaean period.

The corridor opposite this northern group of magazines is

narrowed by a flight of steps on the east side leading to the upper floor (Plan I, 14). In what must have been a cupboard under the stairs was found a group of clay sealings impressed with hieroglyph characters. We proceed north along the corridor as far as the North Terrace wall, from which we can look down on the North Bath or Lustral Area (Plan I, 15) and the Northwest Portico (Plan I, 16). At the point where we are standing (Plan I, 17) Evans made what was represented as one of the most important finds bearing on the absolute chronology of Aegean prehistory. This was a stone lid inscribed with Egyptian hieroglyphs giving the name of the Hyksos king Khyan (see below p. 123). This king is

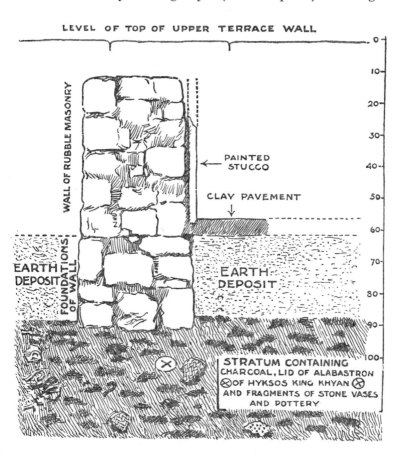

LEVEL OF TOP OF UPPER TERRACE WALL

WALL OF RUBBLE MASONRY

FOUNDATIONS OF WALL

PAINTED STUCCO

CLAY PAVEMENT

EARTH DEPOSIT

EARTH DEPOSIT

STRATUM CONTAINING CHARCOAL, LID OF ALABASTRON OF HYKSOS KING KHYAN AND FRAGMENTS OF STONE VASES AND POTTERY

Fig. 8. *Stratigraphic section in the area of the 'Egyptian Lid' (from the excavation report of 1901).*

datable to about 1630 B.C. In 1901 Evans published[28] an elaborate stratigraphical diagram of the find circumstances on which scholars still rely (see Fig. 8). He stated that the burnt stratum in which the lid was found contained Middle Minoan III B pottery. This is one of the hinge points in Aegean chronology. In fact *The Cambridge Ancient History* states that the lid is the most important evidence for the end of the Early Palace period. However, recent examination of the excavation records has shown that 'Mycenaean' pottery was also collected and stored in the same lot as the Middle Minoan III. Expert opinion[29] has classified one piece as Late Minoan III A : 1, in other words, about 1375 B.C.

Thus the whole of the west quarter, like the West Court, produced consistent evidence that the palace, in its last phase, that is the Late Creto-Mycenaean palace which housed the Linear B tablets, was erected over a burnt stratum containing Late Minoan III pottery.

From the North Terrace wall we now turn south again along the broad passage (Plan I, 18) which runs to the east of the Long Corridor of the Magazines. At the end the passage makes a right-angle turn to the left, and half-way along this east return we come to a doorway. On our left, to the north, lies a block of long, narrow magazines. All these magazines were drastically reconstructed in the Third Late Minoan period.[30] Three of them were blocked with massive cross-walls, which were evidently intended as supports for the upper storey. Thus they resembled the buttresses of the west magazines. In both cases the massive supports in the basement area dating from the Third Late Minoan period imply a major rebuilding during the period ascribed to the 'squatters'.

Beyond the doorway in the passage (Plan I, 19) was found the fine porphyry basin which now stands in the Anteroom to the Throne Room. Evans regarded it as a font for the performance of certain rites by the priest king. Along with the basin was found a 'pilgrim flask' (Fig. 9b), which can be seen in the Archaeological Museum in Herakleion (see below p. 125). There it is exhibited as a typical specimen of the pottery characteristic of the post-palatial period of Crete. Like the porphyry basin associated with it, it stood next to the burnt doorposts of the doorway and so dates the fire which destroyed the Last Palace. It was never reported, and our

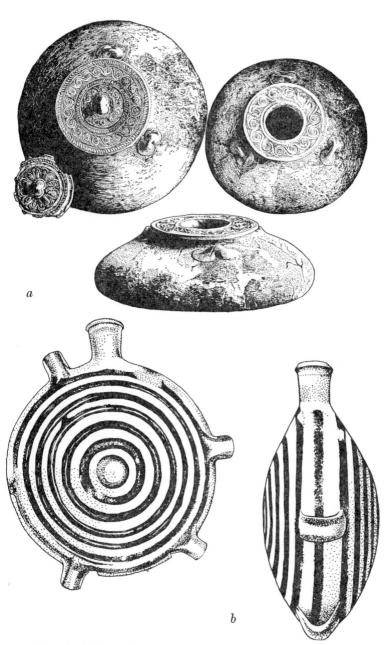

a

b

Fig. 9. *Objects from the Throne Room area:* (a) *carved
alabastra* (after Evans's Palace of Minos)*; (b)* the 'pilgrim
flask' from the Corridor of the Stone Basin.

knowledge of its find place is due to the accurate description which Mackenzie entered in his notebook[31] on the day the passage was excavated. Some Linear B tablets were also found in the debris of the corridor where the flask reposed.

4. The Throne Room Area[32]

Continuing along the passage we emerge in the north-west corner of the Central Court, where the original pavement still survives. To our right lies the Throne Room block. Four steps lead down from the Court to the pavement of the Anteroom (Plan I, 20). This entrance had been partly excavated before Evans arrived on the scene. Stone benches ran along both sides of the Anteroom, with a space on the north side for some wooden article of furniture, perhaps a cupboard. Evans has restored here a chair to match the gypsum throne found in the Throne Room beyond. The throne, with its elaborate carving, was found intact with its top only a few centimetres below the surface. This showed how untouched the site must have been since the destruction of the palace, as Evans remarked in his excavation report of 1900. The doorway in the west wall of the Throne Room was flanked by a fresco showing a couchant griffin wearing a crest of peacock plumes. There was no excavation evidence for the other griffins which were painted in 1930 on either side of the throne (see below).

On the floor of the Throne Room was found a group of fine alabaster vases (Fig. 9a) and an overturned oil jar. It would appear that some ceremony had been in progress when the final blow fell. Important as evidence for the decoration of the ceiling was a large number of glazed roundels. Evans pointed out the close similarity to enamelled plaques from an Egyptian site of the time of Rameses III, that is the beginning of the thirteenth century B.C.* In his 1900 report Evans wrote that there was every reason to suppose that the decoration of the Throne Room belongs to the latest period of the Palace. His dating to the thirteenth century is in accord with what we have found out in the parts of the palace

---

* In an Addendum slip Evans drew attention to what he considered was a closer parallel from the Fourth Shaft Grave at Mycenae. This merely underlines the debility of stylistic comparisons.

so far visited. That date was confirmed by later tests in the Throne Room which were imperfectly reported.

Here at the heart of the palace we can take stock of the problem of Knossos and the violent controversy which it has stirred up. We can also see the great simplicity of the issue and how easy it is to determine what is simply a question of fact. In the *Palace of Minos* Evans relates with much circumstantial detail how difficult he had found it to obtain evidence bearing on the date of the construction of the Throne Room block, which he recognized as a 'revolutionary intrusion' into the architecture of the palace. For years, he wrote, he had carried out tests under the floor — all in vain. At last, in 1913, he raised the great blocks constituting the threshold to the Anteroom. Underneath he found a Late Minoan II sherd. This was evidence, he submitted, which showed that the Throne Room was built during the Late Minoan II period. In fact, even as reported, the evidence merely showed that the threshold had been laid when the vessel represented by this fragment had already been discarded. But the important thing is to decide whether the sherd was correctly classified by Evans. Curiously, despite the great significance attached to it, he never published any illustration of it. Fortunately he drew a sketch of it in his notebook, and recently the material from these crucial tests of 1913 has been rediscovered in the Stratigraphical Museum in Knossos. Expert opinion now assigns the sherd in question to the class Late Minoan III A: 2.[33] In other words, it is characteristic of the 'squatter' period. Yet it was found below the threshold at a point where the surviving part of the pavement of the Central Court fits on to it. This is indicative enough for the late date of the construction of the Throne Room. But examination of the material in the Stratigraphical Museum has revealed that a test had already been carried out in 1903.

The floor of the Anteroom consists of a central section of irregular slabs with a surround of well-cut gypsum slabs. The visitor will note that on the south side two of these slabs have been replaced with modern material. These mark the place of the 1903 test carried out below the pavement. The latest element in the material recovered was the stem of a Late Minoan III goblet.[34] Evidently, the pavement must have been laid after this late material had become stratified. Thus both sets of tests devised to determine the construction date of the Throne Room block produced results which harmonized with those from other parts of the West Wing of the Palace: it was constructed at a time when pottery as late as Late Minoan III A: 2 had already been discarded.

We now enter the Throne Room itself with its carved gypsum throne against the north wall. On the south side opposite the throne is a kind of tank approached by a flight of six steps. There is no outlet to this basin, and it could hardly have been a bath, as some experts have suggested. For why would it have been constructed in this unpractical way by a people who were such experts on drainage? Further, why should a Throne Room have so public a bath? The 'tank' evidently formed an integral part of the Throne Room suite, and the majority of scholars favour the idea that such sunken basins, which are such a feature of Minoan architecture, had some ritual significance. Evans's first idea[35] was that the tank had been originally open to the sky and that it was an ornamental fish tank, a feature with Egyptian affinities. On the north and east walls of the room was painted a landscape showing a stream, on the banks of which grew rushes and sedge-like plants with red flowers. Behind was a background of hills. The river scene, with exotic details such as a palm tree and a fern palm was, in Evans's words, 'obviously suggested by the recurring Nile pieces of contemporary Egyptian art'. None of this can be seen today. Instead a pair of griffins has been painted on either side of the throne. This composition has imposed on modern scholarship despite the account in the excavation report. It has recently been subjected to a minute stylistic analysis by a German expert with a chronological determination much at variance with its true date — A.D. 1930.

Behind the Throne Room lies a set of small service rooms at present barred to the public. The reconstructed upper storey above the Throne Room is wholly modern and imaginative.

We return to the Central Court. The paving of limestone flags can still be seen in this north-west corner (Plan I, 22). Its preservation until the time of the excavation was archaeologically important because it meant that the latest sherds found below it would serve to indicate the date when the pavement was laid. A

Plate III. The Long Corridor of the Magazines as excavated in 1900, looking north. X marks the location of the stratigraphic section drawn in Fig. 6.

number of test pits at intervals between 1904–28, by Mackenzie, Evans and Pendlebury, all yielded the same results. Late Minoan III sherds were among the latest elements and they reached as deep as the second metre below the pavement. An interesting feature of the Central Court at this point has been left exposed to view — the drains which run from the area of the Throne Room in a north-easterly direction towards the main outlet, a capacious stone-built drain which passes under the steeply sloping pavement of the Northern Entrance Passage.

5. The Northern Entrance Passage and the Area of the 'Prisons'[36]

To the north of the Central Court lies one of the most instructive parts of the palace. Here were found in the first year's campaign not only a great mass of Linear B tablets but also some of the most famous works of 'Minoan' art, such as the Bull Relief Fresco, the Miniature Frescoes, and the Saffron Gatherer Fresco. It was in this area, too, that Evans sited the elaborate stratigraphic section which he presented as his sole 'decisive evidence' for dating the Linear B tablets. It is an advantage that the ruins have been left in a state which constitutes a veritable architectural dissection. From it we can read off the successive constructional stages of this ancient building. The following should be consulted: Plan III, reproduced from the excavation report of 1900; Evans's sketch plan, reproduced in Plate VI, which shows the find places of the various objects; and Plate V showing the present state of the site, the photograph having been taken from the floor constructed above the Throne Room.

To survey the scene we take our stance at position X of Plan III. The floor of gypsum slabs (cf. Plate V, 1) at present visible in room Plan III, 2 is not the floor of the Last Palace, which was uncovered in 1900 and afterwards wholly removed. The present floor belongs to an earlier phase of the palace. It will be seen that this lower floor has also been partially removed, revealing the deep pits below which Evans thought might have been used as dungeons — hence his name 'Area of the Prisons'. The following architectural phases can be made out.

The Palace

(1) The cell-like spaces of the 'Prisons' going down as deep as 7 metres constitute the first phase of palace construction. The masonry of the wall, consisting of small blocks of roughly faced limestone, resembles that of the earlier enceinte wall of the palace which enclosed the 'North Bath' (see pp. 63, 79). The spaces left between these walls are too small for the 'cells' to have served as storage pits, as has been suggested. The purpose of this strong close-set system of walls was purely structural. The hill falls away steeply to the north from the plateau constituted by the Central Court, and in order to obtain a platform for the north wing of the palace these walls were sunk deep into a cutting carved out of the hillside. Nothing has been left, so far as can be detected, of the superstructure of this First Palace. But the successive remodellings were unravelled by Mackenzie, whose account I follow.

(2) The first rebuilding is represented by the massive west-east wall (Plate V, 9), the stump of which can be seen in the north-west corner of room Plan III, 2. It rests on one of the 'prison' walls. This wall was cut away when the room in question was laid out with its pavement of fine gypsum slabs, for its foundations were traced out running underneath this pavement.

(3) Thus this pavement represents the third phase of construction. When it was laid, the north wall of the room was built slightly further north (Plate V, 10). This wall, unlike the original north wall, takes no account of the 'prison' wall, its foundations running deep down between the 'prison' walls into one of the 'cells'.

(4) At a still later stage a doorway (Plate V, 6) was made into the room (Plan III, 4) lying north of Plan III, 2, simply by removing some of the blocks of this north wall. There were no door-jambs. At the time this makeshift doorway was made an east wall (Plate V, 11) was also built to room III, 2. That this wall was later than the floor of gypsum slabs was shown when it was established that the edge of the pavement had been broken away when the wall was laid out. On the west side of the room a ramshackle partition wall of miscellaneous material was also erected, resting on a 'prison' wall but slightly askew (Plate V, 5). This wall has been largely removed, but some of its elements can still be seen. The end block was formed by a re-used gypsum

door-jamb (Plate V, 3) placed transversely, and next to it is a large block of rough limestone (Plate V, 4). The space between was originally rammed with clay mortar, but this was removed in the course of exploration. Mackenzie judged this flimsy wall to be a work of the 'reoccupation', and he tested his hunch by digging down alongside it. thirty-two centimetres below the level of the gypsum pavement he found the fragments of an LM II B jar. He duly recorded in his notes that the slanting wall had been built when pottery of the end of the Palace Period had already got stratified.

Mackenzie next turned his attention to the plaster patching of the gypsum paving. This can be seen in the north-west corner of the room (Plate V, 2), and it stretches down through the makeshift doorway (Plate V, 6) into the room to the north (Plate V, 7), where it had also been laid to patch an original floor of gypsum slabs. Mackenzie analysed the plaster and found that its composition was typical of the 'reoccupation' period. This elaborate investigation made it evident that this whole suite of rooms *at this lower level* had been remodelled at a late date, in fact later than the supposed 'final destruction' of the palace qua palace.

(5) How important this finding is will be clear if we recollect that the Last Palace was erected above the floor now visible which we have been studying. This earlier floor level was found covered with about 40 centimetres of debris containing much burnt material. We thus have the same result as in the other parts of the palace — the Last Palace was erected over the ruins of the Penultimate Palace, which had been destroyed by fire during the Late Minoan III period. How drastic the rebuilding was is particularly clear in this part of the site. It will be seen that from point X of Plan III a flight of steps leads down to the earlier floor level of gypsum slabs. These steps were not discovered until 1923. They had been covered up when the Last Palace was built. In fact, they had been partly cut away on the west side, as can be seen, in order to facilitate the laying of the massive foundation block of the building (the hatched block on Plan III) which now rose on the north side of the Central Court. This complete rebuilding, from the foundations up, of the Last Palace is a point of great importance: it will be evident that the finds made above the floor level of this Last Palace, especially the wall frescoes,

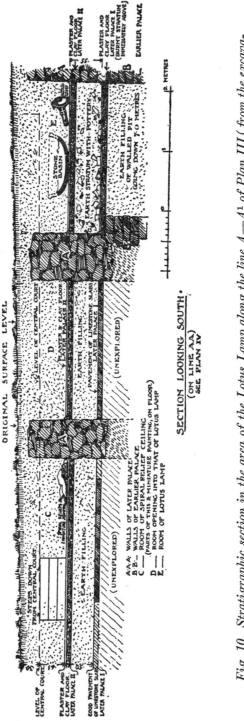

ORIGINAL SURFACE LEVEL

PLASTER AND
CLAY FLOOR
LATER PALACE II

PLASTER AND
CLAY FLOOR
LATER PALACE I
(EARLY STRATUM
IMMEDIATELY ABOVE)

EARLIER PALACE

LEVEL OF CENTRAL COURT

STONE BASIN

D
LATER PALACE II

EARTH FILLING

EARTH STRATUM WITH POTTERY

EARTH FILLING
OF WALLED PIT
GOING DOWN 7·0 METRES

(UNEXPLORED)

B

STEPS DOWN
FROM CENTRAL COURT

E

C

STONE BASIN

A

A

10 METRES

SECTION LOOKING SOUTH.

(ON LINE AA)
SEE PLAN IV

LEVEL OF
CENTRAL COURT

PLASTER AND
CLAY FLOOR
LATER PALACE II

GOOD PAVEMENT
OF LIMESTONE SLABS
LATER PALACE I

(UNEXPLORED)

EARTH FILLING
LATER PALACE I

FRAGMENT OF LIMESTONE SLABS
LATER PALACE

A.A.A. WALLS OF LATER PALACE.
B.B.— WALLS OF EARLIER PALACE.
C — ROOM OF SPIRAL RELIEF CEILING
D — {PARTS OF THIS & MINIATURE PAINTING, ON FLOOR}
D — ROOM OPENING INTO THAT OF LOTUS LAMP
E.— ROOM OF LOTUS LAMP

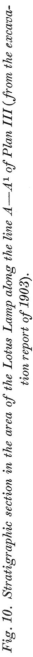

Fig. 10. Stratigraphic section in the area of the Lotus Lamp along the line A—A¹ of Plan III (from the excavation report of 1903).

cannot be attributed to any of the earlier palaces. How important this is we shall see when we come to the famous Saffron Gatherer Fresco, which is regarded as one of the earliest works of 'Minoan' art.

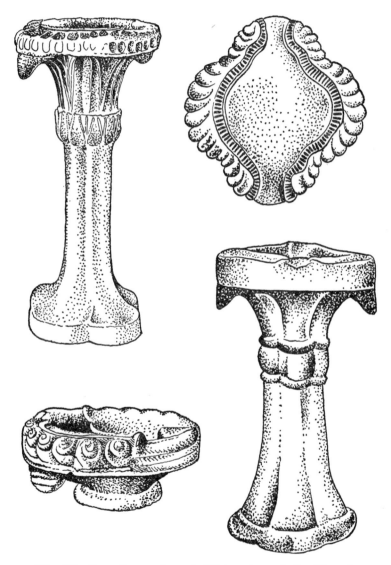

Fig. 11. Stone Lamps from the 'Prisons' area (after Evans's Palace of Minos).

The Palace

It was in 1900, the first year of the excavations, that the floor level of this Last Palace was uncovered lying about 40 centimetres below the pavement of the Central Court on which we are standing and about 40 centimetres above the floor of the Penultimate Palace. When he had removed this topmost floor in later campaigns, Evans published in 1903 a stratigraphic section (Fig. 10) which sets forth the essential facts. In particular it shows the burnt stratum between the two floor levels, which proves that the Penultimate Palace was destroyed by fire. Now that we have unravelled the successive architectural phases of the area of the 'prisons', we can consider the remarkable artistic treasures which were found in 1900 above the floor level of the Last Palace. Plan III will help us to locate them. (6) is the Room of the Spiral Cornice

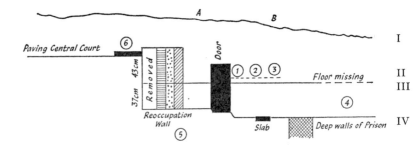

Fig. 12. Stratigraphic section in the 'Prisons' area, along the line B—B¹ of Plan III. A. Room of the Lotus Lamp. Floor level IV examined in 1923; floor patched with late plaster. The slanting west wall perched on the early wall of the 'Prison' is also of LM III date (LM II B sherds found at (5) 32 cm below the level of the gypsum slab floor). (6) south foundation wall of latest construction built over steps descending to floor IV.
B. Room of Saffron Gatherer. Above the floor II, uncovered in 1900, following finds made (cf. Evans's sketch plan Plate VI): (1) and (2) lamps of purple gypsum; (3) Saffron Gatherer Fresco, vase of black steatite, together with Linear B tablets. Floor III of 'cement' was found incomplete in the northern half. Floor IV patched with LM III plaster continuous with that in room A. At (4) some tablets were found in 1901.

(see p. 127), in which were also found the famous Miniature Frescoes (see p. 126); (2) is the Room of the Lotus Lamp, so called after the fine stone lamp which was found there (see Fig. 11 and p. 122); (4) is the Room of the Saffron Gatherer. This fresco was found in 1900 above the floor of the Last Palace which, as we saw, was actually constructed in the Third Late Minoan Period. It is widely regarded, however, as one of the earliest known Minoan frescoes. The reason for this is that in the *Palace of Minos* Evans mistakenly moved the fresco down on to the floor of gypsum slabs, which, despite its patching of LM III plaster, he dated to Middle Minoan II, giving an absolute date of the eighteenth century B.C. to the fresco.

It was in the little room to the west of the Room of the Saffron Gatherer (Plan I, 25; Plan III, 5; Plate V, 8) that Evans sited his elaborate and apparently convincing stratigraphy, which he submitted as 'decisive evidence' for the dating of the Linear B

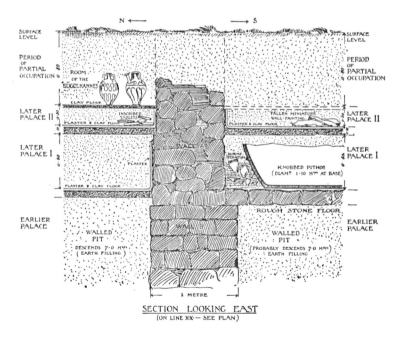

Fig. 13. Evans's stratigraphic section in the Room of the Stirrup-Jars (from the excavation report of 1903), now shown to be a fabrication.

tablets. This room is known as the Room of the Stirrup Jars. Fig. 13 reproduces the section which Evans published in the excavation report for 1903. It runs along the line C–C¹ in Plan III and shows three successive floor levels measured from the surface before excavation. On the top clay floor stirrup-jars with octopus decoration characteristic of the thirteenth century B.C. are sited. Below this comes a floor of plaster and clay on which rests a hoard of Linear B tablets. Finally, below this LM II floor, a third floor is entered and ascribed to a still earlier phase of the Palace.

The records of all three people concerned, Evans, Mackenzie and Fyfe, supported by an examination of the actual remains, have shown that every detail of the section is inaccurate. There were only two floor levels, and the tablets are recorded as lying 'on the clay floor'. Alongside the tablets the late pots were found. In 1935 Evans elaborated the picture still further. He published a photograph purporting to show three of the late pots from the Room of the Stirrup Jars. The pottery notebooks have shown that not one of these vases was found in that room or anywhere near it. Two were found in 1901 on the South Front (see below pp. 110, 112), while the third (the strainer) was found in the west quarter along with the Jewel Fresco and the Vase Tablets (see the section in Fig. 6 on p. 56). Finally, in the same volume Evans published a reproduction of one of the Vase Tablets purporting to come from the Room of the Stirrup Jars. His own Handlist of the tablets has provided the information that in fact it was found near the Southwest Entrance (see above, p. 43). Thus nothing remains of the 'decisive' stratigraphy.

To the east of this set of rooms lies the Northern Entrance Passage (Plan I, 26), which descends steeply northwards from the Central Court. Like the suite of rooms to the west which we have just been inspecting, the passage has a complex architectural history:

(1) When first built, the passage was about seven metres wide.

(2) In the second phase it was narrowed to about two metres by the building of massive walls ('bastions') on either side. This was the state, according to Evans, at the time of the final destruction of the palace. Its paved way is the one now visible.

(3) The 'squatters' pulled down the east bastions and laid an

Plate IV. Magazine XIII as excavated in 1901 showing the superficial cists. Beyond can be seen the 'altar base' and the pavement level of the West Court below which the 'swimming ducks' sherd was found in 1930.

earth roadway about 1·20 metres above the paved way. This earth floor covered up the wall stumps of the dismantled east bastions, and the entrance was now about five metres wide.

This is the account which appears in all the handbooks, including Pendlebury's *Guide*. The curious thing about this account is that all the finds of 1900 were made above the earth floor supposedly laid by the 'squatters', and these finds included one of the most concentrated masses of Linear B tablets. Moreover, we are left in the dark about how the dating of the successive phases was arrived at. To consider the evidence obtained we take our stand on the paved way opposite the passage opening west in which Evans has inserted a modern flight of steps leading up to the reconstructed Bull Relief Fresco (Plan III, 12).

When was the paved way, on which we are standing, laid? In the *Palace of Minos* it is dated to Middle Minoan III A, i.e. the seventeenth century B.C. But no evidence was offered of the usual kind, that is sherds obtained from tests beneath the pavement. It is now known, however, that in 1913 Evans did sink test pits under the pavement at the point where we are standing. Late Minoan II and III pottery was obtained. A further test was carried out by Pendlebury in 1929. He probed under the foundation of the bastion on the east side of the passage at this point. The latest element this time was LM II. Thus both sets of tests gave similar indications, namely that the paved roadway and the bastion had been constructed when LM II–III pottery had already become stratified. But this roadway was a feature of the Penultimate Palace. Above this paved way, as has been said, was an earth road belonging to the last occupation of the palace site. This was about chest high as we stand on the pavement (1·20 metres). Resting on the surface of the earth road and stretching along it to our right as far as the spur of wall (Plan III, 8) was a deposit of Linear B tablets (Plan III, 9–9[1]) so vast that Evans sent an excited telegram to his father. The tablets were intimately associated with a large deposit of double vases of Late Minoan III B date. As we shall see (p. 124), some of these are now exhibited in the Post-Palatial room of the Archaeological Museum. To our left, to the south of the little passage opening before us, and close to the original surface before excavation, which was about three and a half metres above the paved way, another group of Linear B tablets lay together with the remains of the container and a large clay seal impression with which it had been sealed (Plan III, 10, 11). Evans rightly concluded that they had fallen into this position from a room overlooking the Entrance Passage. We add that the fall must have taken place after the earth floor was laid. Again, considerably above the LM III earth floor the remnants of a famous work of 'Minoan' art were found. This was the Bull Relief Fresco, a replica of which is mounted in the reconstructed Portico.

The section (Fig. 14) taken along the Line D–D¹ of Plan III shows the stratification of all these important finds, which are entered also on Evans's sketch plan (Plate VI). It is thus clear, that apart from the Linear B tablets compiled by the clerks of the Mycenaean kings of Knossos, the following works of art belong to this Last Palace: the Lotus Lamp and another stone lamp

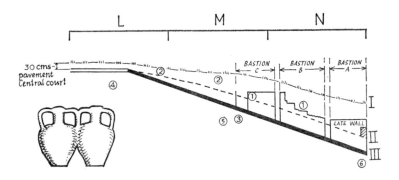

Fig. 14. Stratigraphic section in the Northern Entrance Passage, along the line D—D¹ of Plan III. I surface before excavation. II earth floor with late walls resting on it, uncovered in 1900. III paved floor uncovered in 1901. (1) Great Deposit of tablets found along with LM III B double jars; (2) surface deposit of tablets along with 'Great Seal'; (3) LM II and III sherds discovered under floor III by Evans in 1913; (4) LM III sherds found below pavement of Central Court in 1928; (5) LM II sherd found by Pendlebury in 1929 below the foundations of a bastion; (6) LM III sherds (1929).

(Fig. 11), the Spiral Cornice, the Miniature Frescoes, the Saffron Gatherer Fresco, and the Bull Relief Fresco. We shall see all these in the Archaeological Museum (see below pp. 126 f.). The stratification, as summarized in the section Fig. 14, shows that all these artistic products belong to the Creto-Mycenaean Palace built over the burnt ruins of the Penultimate Palace, which itself had been constructed when LM II–III pottery had already become stratified. Their intimate association with Late Minoan III B pots shows that they are datable at the earliest to the thirteenth century B.C.

We now descend the Entrance Passage. Notable features are the fine ashlar masonry of the walls and the capacious stone drain that runs under the paved way and carries the discharge from a drain running across the Central Court north-east from the Throne Room area. At the bottom of the Entrance Passage is a Pillar Hall (Plan I, 27). In the latest phase of the Palace this had been much built up with late walls, which have been removed in the course of excavation.

Turning left, that is west, we pass the Northwest Portico (Plan I, 16) and come to the North Lustral Basin (Plan I, 15). This is a structure of much the same character as the 'tank' flanking the Throne Room. Here, too, the more likely explanation is that the building had some ritual significance. This whole area lying outside the north terrace wall of the Last Palace, belongs to an earlier palace, and when the Last Palace was built, it had become choked with debris and overlaid with later constructions. At a point opposite the Long Corridor of the Magazines, as we look south, we can see where the famous Egyptian lid was found (see above p. 63). The later structure and floor below which it was found have been removed. One point of architectural interest may be recalled here: when the Lustral Basin was in use it was enclosed by an earlier enceinte wall. Apropos of this wall Mackenzie noted that the masonry of small stones was the same as that of the 'Prisons', and he concluded that these structures were contemporary. The enceinte wall was later replaced by a wall lying much further south — the still existing north terrace wall of the Last Palace.

We continue west and come up to the so-called Theatral Area

The Palace

(Plan I, 28). This lies north of the West Court, flanking the North-west Treasure House (see above p. 38). A small area paved with flags is bordered by flights of steps on the south and east sides. At the junction of the two sets of steps stands a massive square structure, which Evans considered to be the base of a royal 'box'. The steps are evidently not part of an approach to the palace, since the paved way leading to the Northern Entrance skirts it on the south side (see Plan I). Evans believed that this was a primitive theatre in which the spectators stood on the steps to watch spectacles performed on the paved rectangle. He identified this whole structure with the dancing place which the wonder builder Daedalus built for Ariadne. In 1903 he greeted the veteran archaeologist Dr Dörpfeld, the collaborator of Schliemann, who was conducting a party of tourists, by staging here a dance performed by his Cretan workmen and their womenfolk.

A paved way — the Royal Road — leads westwards from the centre of the east flight of steps. This continues down the slope, and at the bottom, about a hundred metres from the steps, Evans found the remains of the burnt-out arsenal. This yielded boxes of bronze arrow heads and Linear B tablets recording bodies and wheels of chariots. A point of archaeological interest is that clay sealings were found along with the boxes, and they bore the impression of a seal showing a lion couchant. This gives us an important archaeological cross-reference, for an impression from the same seal was found with other armament records recovered from the south-east corner of the palace — the Sword Tablets. This point will be discussed when we reach this part of the site (see p. 105).

6. THE DOMESTIC QUARTER[37]

We now retrace our steps up the Northern Entrance Passage and walk to the east side of the Central Court (following the arrows on Plan I).* Here is one of the most impressive monuments of Minoan architecture: the Grand Staircase (Plan I, 29), which gives access to the residential part of the palace, called by Evans the Domestic Quarter. The space for this wing was created by making

* See also Plan IV, drawn on a larger scale.

a deep cutting in the hillside to the east of the Central Court, so that two floors of this part of the palace lie below the level of the Court. The building possibly rose another two storeys above it.

Throughout this part of the palace the signs of a gigantic conflagration were particularly apparent. In the early days of 1900, when Evans was first reconnoitring the site before beginning the excavation proper, he noted on this east side the charred beams and other signs of fire on the surface. When he excavated the Domestic Quarter in 1901–2, he found that the deposit was crowned with charred wood from the roof timbering. Underneath was a concrete-hard deposit due to the action of moisture on the powdered 'plaster of Paris' produced by the action of the blaze on the gypsum stonework. Below this was a looser deposit reaching down to the floor. The Grand Staircase itself had been particularly affected by the fierce heat because of the updraught.

It is well to insist on these points, because Evans repeatedly declared that the Domestic Quarter had been comparatively unaffected by the great 'final' destruction of 1400 B.C. (on his computations). He wrote that after the great disaster the Domestic Quarter continued to be inhabited by 'dynasts of diminished status'. Much the same was concluded by Pendlebury. In 1939, after a thorough survey of the pottery evidence, to which his own tests had added, he wrote in his authoritative book *The Archaeology of Crete* that the Domestic Quarter had been completely cleared of debris after the disaster of Late Minoan II and re-inhabited with little or no alteration. This naturally implied that the destruction debris actually found by the excavators could hardly have been that which had been 'completely cleared away'. It must have marked the end of the epoch of 'the diminished dynasts'. Thus the 'reoccupied' Domestic Quarter must also have met its end in a disastrous fire. These historical and archaeological puzzles will multiply as we explore the Domestic Quarter.

Before we descend, the general lay-out of this quarter may be noted with the help of Plan I. The staircase received its light from a light-well, the Hall of the Colonnade (Plan I, 30). To the east of this, that is straight ahead as we look from the Court, lies the grandest of the apartments, the Hall of the Double Axes (Plan I, 31), which is flanked on the north by the main corridor, the East-

West Corridor (Plan I, 32). To the south, that is to the right of the light-well I, 30, lies a more secluded suite, the Queen's Megaron (Plan I, 33) and its service rooms. The main East-West Corridor, at its east end (Plan I, 44) turns left, that is north, and leads to a block of important workrooms concerned with technical activities such as stone carving.

We now descend the staircase to the Upper East-West Corridor. On the landing here was found a pile of clay sealings, while a great mass of tablets stretched east along the corridor. These documents recorded flocks of sheep with named shepherds and their locations. It is from these texts that we get some idea of the extent of the territory closely controlled by the King of Knossos. His domains evidently included virtually the whole of Crete. A gallery runs round the east side of the light well at the upper floor level, and here Evans has placed a replica of the Shield Fresco (Plan I, 34). The fragments were few and they were in any case found in the stair-well on the south side of the Hall of the Colonnade (Plan I, 35). Evans recontructed the fresco on the model of the better preserved Shield Fresco at Tiryns (thirteenth century B.C.). This latter was then declared to be an imitation of the Knossos fresco, which was dated by Evans to the fifteenth century B.C.

From the landing of the staircase we descend further to the ground floor of the Hall of the Colonnade and pass through the doorway in the south-east corner. Immediately on our right is a staircase (Plan I, 35) with two flights, first up west and then with a return up east. This is archaeologically one of the most important parts of the palace. Evans found only the stair-well, but the position of the steps was indicated by stone supports. He concluded that the steps must have been of wood — hence his name for it the Wooden Stairs.

Only the north half of the stair-well was excavated in 1901. Here were found a large number of clay sealings including some impressed with a 'daemon'. Along with the Daemon Seals were also found the fragments of the Shield Fresco, while just to the north, at a high level in the deposit of the Hall of the Colonnade, the largest Linear B tablet found on the site turned up. It bore a list of names, and one of them recurred on the tablet found near the 'South-West Door' (Plan I, 1). Both tablets were written by the same scribe (see above, p. 43), and this gives us yet another archaeological cross-reference. In 1902 the southern half of the Wooden Stairs was excavated. Again, masses of clay sealings were recovered. They lay along the upper flight of stairs and none occurred lower than the landing halfway up. This was an important finding, as can be seen from the section in Fig. 15. The space underneath the upper flight of stairs had been used as a cupboard. On its floor were standing a number of intact vessels, including a stirrup-jar with the conventionalized octopus decoration of the 'period of decadence', as Evans called it. Evidently, the sealings

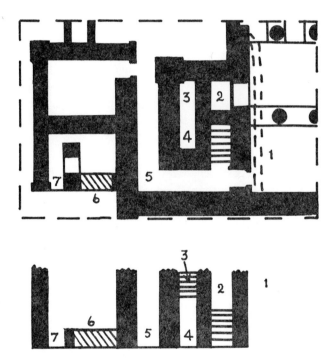

Fig. 15. Plan and stratigraphic section in the area of the Wooden Stairs: (1) the Great Tablet; (2) Daemon Seals and Shield Fresco; (3) seals on upper flight of stairs; (4) stair cupboard with LM III B vessels on floor; (5) seals on floor of corridor; (6) seals and LM III B stirrup-jars at level of balustrade in Queen's Bathroom; (7) late jar at entrance to passage leading to Queen's Bathroom.

had fallen from above on to the stairs in the same destruction that had engulfed the late vessels in their cupboard below the stairs.

Some of the sealings belonging to this deposit had been spilled over the balustrade of the Queen's Bathroom, which lies a little to the south (Plan I, 40). They were also found together with Late Minoan III B stirrup-jars. At this point we shall be in the position of eye-witnesses, for Evans took a photograph at the time of excavation (see below). It is clear that these sealings and tablets belonged to the same period as the stirrup-jars found together with and below them in the same destruction debris. The same is true of the Shield Fresco, and this is likely to be later than the Tiryns Fresco, which Evans used as a model for restoring the Knossos fragments.

A few steps after passing the Wooden Stairs (which have been restored in stone) the passage takes a turn to the right, and we pass on the left a dark secluded chamber (Plan I, 36) which is labelled Archive of Inscribed Tablets (but not a single tablet was found in it). This is the room dubbed by Evans 'the Lair'. At this point, but on the upper floor level, late stirrup-jars were also found, and some of them had been hurled down over the balustrade of the Queen's Bathroom, which adjoins it on the east side (see below). This turn of the passage is lit by a light-well immediately ahead; it is called the Court of the Distaffs from the mason's marks on the walls (Plan I, 37). The Court also gives light to a room on the south side which has a plaster couch in the corner (Plan I, 38). This little room is remarkable for its latrine. This is a little closet with slight walls of thin gypsum slabs and a floor of the same material. There is a slot along the back wall which discharges into the main drainage system which we shall discuss below. There was probably a wooden seat mounted over the slot. There is yet another opening into the drain in the floor just outside the closet. This toilet room, where perhaps a servant slept on the plaster couch, belongs to the Queen's Megaron (Plan I, 33).

We approach this apartment along a corridor running east (Plan I, 39). At the mouth of this corridor as we emerge was found a painted jar, which now stands in the north-west corner of the Queen's Megaron against the balustrade of the little inner room (the 'Bathroom'). The jar is classified by archaeologists as Late Minoan I A (sixteenth century) and it was found filled with 'lime'. The oddity of this fact will appear in a moment.

The Queen's Megaron (Plan I, 33) is a spacious room lighted through balustrades giving on to light-wells on the east and south sides. A portico faces the east light-well. In front of the balustrade are benches. An opening alongside the corridor from which we have just emerged leads to an inner room (Plan I, 40), which also received its light through a balustrade. At the time of the excavation in 1902 a late jar stood in this entrance, and it too was filled with 'lime'. Evans called this inner room the Queen's Bathroom, and he has placed in it a fine decorated bath tub. However, this was not actually found there but in the east light-well. Possibly this inner room was used as an alcove or bedroom.

If we now stand in the south-east corner of the Queen's Megaron, that is diagonally opposite the corner where the jar painted with spirals now stands, we can survey the finds. Of prime importance, of course, is the pottery. Fortunately, at the time of excavation a photograph was taken from the place where we are now standing.[38] It shows a workman standing alongside the as yet unexcavated side of the section against the balustrade of the 'bathroom'. In the debris upside down several Late Minoan III B stirrup-jars can be seen.* Now, elsewhere Evans informs us that some of the clay sealings from the room above the 'Lair' (immediately west of the bathroom) had been spilled down over the balustrade of the bathroom. Moreover, a late jar, as we saw above, was actually standing in the door alongside the balustrade. We can now add still another fact concerning the pottery found in this area which Evans communicates in yet another place of his great work. He stated that a vast quantity of the late goblets called 'champagne cups' had been found in the south-east part of the palace stretching as far as the staircase of the Queen's Megaron (this can be seen in the north wall facing us). There can be no doubt, therefore, that the Queen's Megaron area, like the Wooden Stairs, had been in occupation when Late Minoan III B pots were in use. Other evidence was to show that the building had been actually

---

* One of these jars has been identified in the Museum stores by a French expert, J. Raison.

a

Fig. 16. Frescoes from the area of the Queen's Megaron:
(a) the Dolphin Fresco; (b) the Dancing Girl.

b

reconstructed when some Late Minoan III B pottery had already
been discarded. This was doubtless part of the evidence which led
Evans to conclude that there had been signs of large-scale
reconstruction in the Domestic Quarter.

We can best approach this evidence by following up the
Dolphin Fresco (Fig. 16a), a replica of which has been placed on
the wall opposite us. Evans stated that it had been found with
fifteenth-century sherds, but he dated its composition to Middle
Minoan III B (seventeenth century B.C.). The find facts were
different. The fragments of the fresco were found on the far (i.e.
east) side of the east wall of the east light-well (Plan I, 42). In
other words, it was found above the surface of the south light-well
of the Hall of the Double Axes (see below). On the near side of the
wall, in the east light-well of the Queen's Megaron (Plan I, 41),
there was a great pile of Late Minoan III B stirrup-jars, which
were duly recorded both by Mackenzie and Evans. Thus the
associations of the Dolphin Fresco were clearly Late Minoan III
B. Only two scraps of Late Minoan II were found. In his publication Evans singled these out for mention but omitted to report
the mass of late stirrup-jars. But more surprising evidence was
obtained later.

The 'Fish Fresco', as it was called at the time of excavation,
was found above the concrete floor of the light-well (Plan I, 42).
Later tests showed that this concrete had actually been laid
during the Late Minoan III B period (see below). But at the
moment we are concerned with the Queen's Megaron. In the north
wall opposite us are two doorways. The one on the right leads to a
flight of stairs — the so-called Private Staircase. At different
times probes were made under the top step and under the seventh
step. From inside the masonry of the staircase Late Minoan II
and Late Minoan III sherds were obtained. Thus the now familiar
pattern of evidence was repeated: the tablets, the clay sealings,
and the various artistic treasures of the Last Palace belonged to a
building occupied when Late Minoan III B jars were in use. The
building was actually constructed when sherds of the Third
Late Minoan class had already become stratified and incorporated
in the masonry.

Before leaving the Queen's Megaron we may consider a piece of archaeological deduction advanced by Evans. The two jars found, as we saw, side by side in adjacent passages on the west side of the room were filled with 'lime' at the time of excavation. The 'Bathroom' itself contained a great quantity of the same substance, and piles of it were found here and there throughout this area. Evans deduced from this that decorators had been at work when the final blow fell. It appeared that they had pressed the two jars into service as lime containers. To explain the heaps of frescoes found on the floor, Evans suggested that they had just been picked from the walls preparatory to replastering. The presumed decorators had fled, taking their tools with them.

There are some difficulties about this story. In the first place this decoration must have been the work of the 'diminished dynasts', who in Evans's account continued to inhabit the Domestic Quarter for centuries after the great destruction of 1400 B.C. (see above, p. 81). But such piles of 'lime' were also found in the Hall of the Double Axes, which comes next in the tour. Here a pile of 'lime' was actually found heaped over the remains of the wooden throne. Some exclude this room from the reoccupation. But then it would be a simple coincidence that the Late Minoan II Palace was also undergoing redecoration at the time of its destruction. And would decorators throw a pile of lime over the throne? The explanation of the 'lime' deposits is much simpler and was given by Mackenzie. Gypsum, under the action of heat, has its water content driven out and is reduced to plaster of Paris. Thus the 'lime' was simply a consequence of the fierce blaze which destroyed the palace. It was one and the same fire which raged in the Hall of the Double Axes and the adjoining Queen's Megaron. That fire is dated by the Late Minoan III B stirrup-jars and other pottery of the same period found so abundantly in the ruins.

We may now leave the Queen's Megaron by the left-hand door in the north wall. We enter a passage lined with gypsum slabs that are blackened by fire. The passage takes a turn to the right and then again to the left. We emerge into the Hall of the Double Axes (Plan I, 31), so-called from the mason's marks visible on the walls of the light-well on the west side. This is a magnificent hall measuring some 8 × 12 m. The floor consists of a central rectangle composed of slabs of unequal size. This is surrounded by a border of gypsum slabs laid in a regular pattern. The walls were decorated with a dado of thin gypsum sheets with painted plaster above. The western section of the room has a two-column portico facing a light-well.

There is access into the east section of the hall through a system of four doorways between three oblong piers with double reveals and two half-piers against the two walls. This is matched by a similar system some 5·40 m to the east. Here the north wall of the hall continues for another 5·80 m and forms the side wall of a paved portico facing the east light-well. On the south side a similar system with three doorways gives on to another portico facing the south light-well. This elaborate system of doors acted as partly movable partitions which made the hall adaptable to different climatic conditions. The openings could be closed by folding doors, as is indicated by pivot holes in the floor. Such 'pier-and-door' partitions are a familiar feature of Minoan palaces and houses.

The light-well is also a common feature of Minoan architecture, and there are no fewer than five in this quarter of the palace. It is a device which provides ample ventilation and light but excludes draughts and direct sunshine. The light-wells were open to the sky and were provided with a waterproof surface. The material used for this purpose was what Evans called 'terrazza'. This consisted of lime plaster mixed with tiny pebbles. Archaeologically this is of particular interest and importance. Such a cement surface effectively creates a 'sealed deposit' below it. The latest sherds found below such a surface give a *terminus post quem* for the laying of the 'terrazza'.

A number of such tests were made in the east and south light-wells of the Hall of the Double Axes. Late Minoan III B material was secured as deep as 2 m below the concrete. But in 1929 there was a still more drastic test. This time it was carried out by Pendlebury, who was Evans's assistant at the time. He dug under the foundations of the east wall of the east light-well. Once again LM III sherds were found. Going now into the south light-well (Plan I, 42), we may remind ourselves that on the far side of the west wall is the light-well of the Queen's Megaron. On the near side of the wall were found not only the fragments of the Dolphin

Fresco but also the delightful 'Dancing Girl' (Fig. 16b). On the other side of the wall was the great pile of LM III B stirrup-jars. The terrazza under our feet sealed in Late Minoan III B sherds. There can be no doubt about the date of these famous works of 'Minoan' art found above the terrazza: they are Creto-Mycenaean products of the thirteenth century B.C.

The Domestic Quarter also offers a fine example of a Minoan drainage system. Stone shafts descended from upper floors and discharged waste water into a conduit built of stone blocks lined with cement. This conduit, which was covered with flat slabs, is about one metre high and half a metre wide, so that a man could easily make his way along it for cleaning purposes. The course of the drains in the Domestic Quarter is shown in broken lines on Plan I. One branch starts below the shaft located south of the Queen's WC (Plan I, 38) and runs under the south light-well of the Queen's Megaron (Plan I, 33). Under the south light-well of the Hall of the Double Axes (Plan I, 42) it is joined by another branch with its highest point under the Court of the Distaffs (Plan I, 37). Thence it receives the drainage of the Hall of the Colonnade (Plan I, 30) and next that of the west light-well of the Hall of the Double Axes (West of Plan I, 31). From this point on the drain is large enough for a man to crawl along. After the confluence in the south light-well of the Hall of the Double Axes (Plan I, 42), where a section is exposed to view, another tributary enters running from the north along the foundations of the east wall. The drain discharged down the east slope beyond this point.

We leave the Hall of the Double Axes by a doorway in the north wall of the east light-well and find ourselves at the foot of a staircase (Plan I, 43) leading up to the Upper East-West Corridor. Exceptional importance attaches to the suite of rooms which faces us on the north side of the staircase.[39] Fortunately the successive excavations are minutely documented. Plan IV and the section in Fig. 17 (taken along the line A–A¹ on the plan) should be consulted. I take the rooms in order from south to north. First comes the Room of the Wooden Posts (Plan I, 45). Evans has reconstructed this in concrete coloured to represent the wood-work which gives the room its name. The centre post still supports a large block of stone which at the start of the excavation was

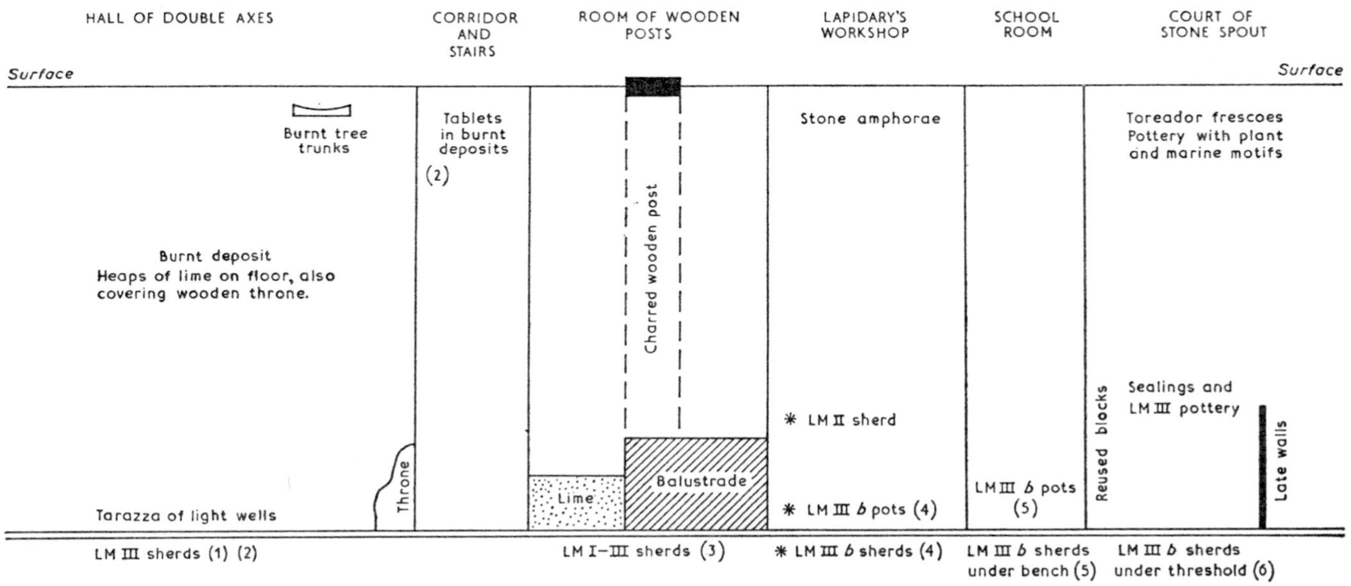

Fig. 17. Stratigraphic section in the area of the School Room. Note the LM III B sherds below floors overlaid with fire debris.

visible above the ground. This block can be seen if you ascend the flight of stairs to the Upper Corridor. It was at this point (Plan IV, 1, Plan I, 44) that the first of the Linear B 'sheep tablets' was found on the floor of the Corridor, the deposit stretching as a dense mass towards the landing of the Grand Staircase at the west end. At this point, too, at the upper floor level, above the Room of the Wooden Posts, were found some of the most striking works of Minoan art. These were parts of human figures in high relief and other subjects, including a sphinx. Of particular interest was a left forearm with a hand holding a pointed vase. Evans waxed enthusiastic over the modelling of the muscles and the veins, and he wrote of the artistic perfection achieved in these coloured reliefs. Immediately south of this point (Plan I, 44), in the fill of the Hall of the Double Axes, the excavators found at this high level a half-burnt tree trunk. From this we know both the type of wood used for such pillars (cypress) and their shape. So much for the objects found at the level of the Upper East-West Corridor in the fire debris.

On working his way below the large block of stone, which acted as a landmark at the time of the excavation, Evans found that it was supported in position merely by the fallen debris which had choked the room below. He built a scaffolding to support it in position and took a photograph, which is in the Ashmolean Museum at Oxford. Underneath the block of stone Evans was able to trace the charred remains of a wooden post. When he reached the lower floor, which was paved with limestone slabs, he found that it was covered deep with 'lime' produced by the action of the fire on the gypsum stone used in the construction (see above, p. 88). Here, once again, was indisputable evidence of fire debris left undisturbed since the great destruction. For an archaeologist it was vital to know what was the latest pottery found under the pavement of limestone slabs, thus covered by the results of the conflagration. It is now known from Evans's private notebook that in 1905 he did make a test in the Room of the Wooden Posts. His record shows that among the sherds he obtained were some of the Late Minoan III class. It goes without saying that the test of 1905 must have been under the pavement that had been cleared in 1901.

The Palace

The evident implication that this part of the building had actually been *constructed* when pottery of this late type had already become stratified was confirmed again and again by other tests made in this area at various dates. From the Room of the Wooden Posts we enter the corridor (Plan IV, 2) which runs as a north return of the Lower East-West Corridor. Evans found it blocked by a crosss-wall which turned the northern part of the Corridor into a magazine (Plan IV). In this magazine, ranged against the west wall, stood a variety of vessels of Late Minoan III B type. Of great significance was that they stood along the charred remains of wall posts, the sockets of which can still be seen in the wall. These late pots, marking the final period of occupation, date the fire. We may be reminded of the late 'pilgrim flask' alongside the burnt doorposts in the Throne Room Corridor (see above, p. 64).

But what of the final phase of *construction*? In order to ascertain this Evans proceeded in the usual archaeological way: he dismantled the blocking wall and found that the masonry contained Late Minoan III sherds. In the third volume of the *Palace of Minos* he frankly admitted that this whole suite of rooms had been reconstructed in the Third Late Minoan period and, what is more during the final phase of that period — Late Minoan III B. The evidence he offered for that conclusion we shall see in a moment. But it is the next room, on the right of the corridor (Plan IV, 3; Plan I, 47), that offers significant information bearing on the cultural level of the palace at this late period of occupation (Evans's 'squatterdom') and on its foreign relations. On the ground floor the visitor will still see blocks of stone used by stone carvers. This is Spartan basalt, *lapis lacedaemonius,* obtainable only from a site near Sparta on the Greek mainland. Here we have evidence of importation of luxury material at the time when Crete was supposed to have been a quiet backwater cut off from world commerce. No less significant were the finds made in the stone-mason's room above his store of Spartan basalt. Within 25 cm of the surface Evans unearthed two magnificent carved stone jars (Fig. 18a). They were in an unfinished state. This is a fact of great importance, since stone vases may last for centuries and this means that stylistic evidence for date of manufacture cannot be taken as evidence for the date of deposit. But as Evans pointed

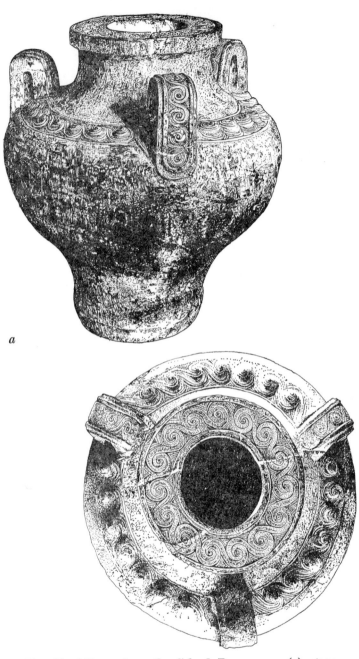

a

Fig. 18. Objects from the School Room area: (a) stone
amphora (after Evans's Palace of Minos); (b) (opposite)
the Toreador Fresco.

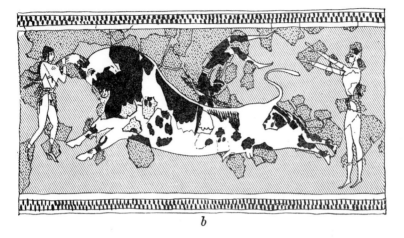

b

out the stone carvers must have been disturbed in their work when
the great fire destroyed the Palace. The jars are thus indisputable
evidence for contemporary products of the Last Palace in its final
moments, that is at the end of Late Minoan III B. These jars also
give us an important archaeological cross-reference. Evans himself drew attention to the striking stylistic similarity between the
stone jars found in the workshop here and the alabaster vessels
found on the floor of the Throne Room (see p. 66 and Fig. 9a).
In both find places it was clearly established by probes below the
pavement that the last phase of the construction of the rooms in
question took place in Late Minoan III times.

Evans obtained further confirmation for his conclusion that the
rebuilding of this part of the palace was entirely the work of the
Third Minoan Period and 'carried out indeed not earlier than its
final phase' (as he wrote in the *Palace of Minos*) when he investi-
gated the room which lies on the north side of the store of
sculptor's material (Plan IV, 4; Plan I, 48). He called this room
the School Room, because of the benches running along the wall.
It faces on to a courtyard, named the Court of the Stone Spout
(Plan IV, 5; Plan I, 50), so-called from the spout which projects
from its west wall. The School Room (now labelled the Potter's
Workshop) had a small inner room (Plan I, 49) in which stood a
number of complete Late Minoan III B vessels on a bench
constructed of rubble masonry built against the west wall. Here,

too, it proved that Late Minoan III B occupation had been proceeded by Late Minoan III construction. Evans dismantled the rubble bench and found LM III sherds incorporated in the masonry.

Thus far the evidence as submitted and recorded in the notebook and published in the *Palace of Minos* had shown merely undifferentiated LM III sherds below the floors and inside the masonry. There was as yet no distinction between LM III A and LM III B. How late the date of the last construction of these rooms had been was not revealed to Evans until 1929. The School Room has a doorway opening on to the Court of the Stone Spout. The threshold consists of a single block of stone weighing over a ton. When Evans had it lifted, he found underneath pedestal cups of the latest Late Minoan III B type. He could no longer doubt that the actual reconstruction of this whole set of rooms belongs to the later phase of what he believed the 'squatter' period. This admission and retraction he published in the third volume of the *Palace of Minos*.

By now Evans was eighty years old, and he seems not to have realized the implications of his change of mind under the impact of the new evidence. If the whole set of rooms had been rebuilt at so late a date, then evidently their contents must be still later. In 1901 the Court of the Stone Spout had yielded at a high level in the deposit one of the most famous works of 'Minoan' art. This was the Toreador Fresco, which shows a man somersaulting over the back of a charging bull (Fig. 18b). If we take our stance at point 50 of Plan I and look south towards this set of rooms, we can review the finds. The stratigraphy is set forth in the section Fig. 17. Just to our left is the entrance to the School Room, under the threshold block of which fragmentary LM III B cups were found, while beyond to our left is the inner room where stood the LM III B vessels on a bench which had LM III sherds incorporated in its masonry. In the court where we are standing small chambers of rubble masonry had been built up against the fine terrace wall on our right. All this has been removed. High above our heads was found the Toreador Fresco. On our right is the passage leading south from the School Room, where the complete LM III B jars were found standing against the wall with its charred wall

Plate V. The area of the 'Prisons' seen from the floor above the
Throne Room: (1) pavement of the Penultimate Palace; (2) plaster
patching on gypsum slab floor; (3) re-used gypsum door-jamb;
(4) limestone block; (5) 'Prison' wall on which late wall rests;
(6) doorway into Room of Saffron Gatherer; (7) Room of Saffron
Gatherer; (8) Room of Stirrup-Jars; (9) earlier north wall of Room
of Lotus Lamp with foundations running under gypsum slab floor;
(10) later wall of Room of Lotus Lamp; (11) east wall of Room of
Lotus Lamp; (12) reconstructed portico of Bull Relief.

posts. In the room on the left of the passage was the store of Spartan basalt and high above it, within 25 cm of the surface, were found the splendid carved stone jars, still unfinished. Beyond this was the Room of the Posts with the high reliefs at the top floor level and the LM III sherds below the limestone paving of the ground floor room, covered as it was with the burnt 'lime'. Immediately beyond, at the beginning of the Upper East-West Corridor, began the extensive deposit of Linear B tablets. At the same high level, in the deposit of the Hall of the Double Axes, was the burnt tree trunk.

This massive concentration of carefully recorded evidence makes it plain that all the famous works of 'Minoan' art found in this set of rooms belong to the Late Creto-Mycenaean Palace, the construction date of which is indicated by the Late Minoan III B material found below its floors.

To the west of the School Room complex, Plan I shows a rectangle of massive foundation walls extending as far as the Central Court. To approach this rectangle of rooms, which are situated at the upper floor level to the west of the terrace wall, we leave the Court of the Stone Spout by an opening on its north side. In front of us is a store of huge jars — the Magazine of the Giant Pithoi (Plan I, 51). Below us to our right lies the East Bastion, which is worth a visit because of the clever way in which the flow of rainwater down the steep slope was controlled. The runnel alongside the steps is constructed as a series of shallow waterfalls, so that the speed of flow is checked just before the right-angle turns. The masonry of the East Bastion showed a late addition which gives a cross-reference to the extreme west side of the palace (see below, p. 113).

From the East Bastion we retrace our steps past the Giant Pithoi and ascend the steps leading up first west and then south and we find ourselves in the Corridor of the Draughtboard (Plan I, 52). Evans gave it this name because of the magnificent inlaid gaming board in ivory and crystal which he found here in the sur-face deposit. This board is exhibited in the Archaeological Museum (see below, p. 121). Noteworthy are the sections of terra-cotta pipes laid under the pavement of the corridor. These are not simple waste pipes, like those under the bathroom in the South

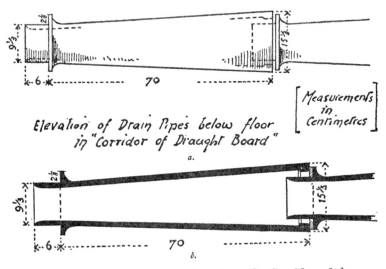

Elevation of Drain Pipes below floor in "Corridor of Draught Board"

a.

Measurements in Centimetres

b.

Fig. 19. Terracotta water pipes from the Corridor of the Draughtboard (from the excavation report of 1901).

Propylaeum Area (see p. 49), but they are constructed ingeniously so as to resist the pressure of water. Fig. 19 shows that the mouth-piece of each tube is provided with a stop-ridge which prevented its being forced into the butt end of the adjacent tube and so splitting it. The inside of the butt is provided with a corresponding raised collar which offers a widened area to the pressure of the stop-ridge. Schliemann's collaborator Dörpfeld reported pipes of similar construction from a site on the island of Leucas.

The area round the Corridor of the Draughtboard offered much evidence of occupation in Late Minoan III B times. This appears in the notebooks of both Evans and Mackenzie. On the west side of the corridor is the North-East Hall (Plan I, 53), with a two-column portico at its north end. From this point we can look north-west towards the Northern Entrance Passage with the Bull Relief Fresco across a set of small rooms known as the North-East Magazines (Plan I, 54).

We now turn south along the Corridor of the Draughtboard and enter the 'rectangle' referred to above. We should note that in the first year's excavation of this part (1901) evidence was secured of LM III B occupation in the shape of stores of pottery. These were found in various places including the south-east corner (adjacent to Plan I, 44) where the high reliefs were found extending into the space over the Room of the Wooden Posts (Plan I, 45). We recall that this room was constructed when LM III sherds had become stratified. The importance of this finding will become apparent in a moment when we come to the Magazine of the Medallion Pithoi.

From the Corridor of the Draughtboard we enter first a room (Plan I, 55) with a shallow trough, from which a runnel finds a devious route towards the stone spout in the court we have just left. Evans at first believed that the trough was part of an olive press. The runnel, a few metres after leaving the trough, discharges into a rectangular settling basin. Later Evans came to believe that all was part of a system for carrying off rainwater. But there are other installations of this kind in Crete and Evans may well have been right in his first diagnosis in the 'Room of the Olive Press' as he called it.

West of this room is the elongated Magazine of the Medallion Pithoi (Plan I, 56), so-called from the large jars (restored from fragments) which are now placed there. Pendlebury's *Guide* comments obscurely: 'They [the pithoi] are mainly important for the light they shed on a particularly debatable point in the history of Mycenae'. This point may be made explicit. It is an allusion to Evans's dispute with the Cambridge archaeologist Wace about the date of the beehive tombs at Mycenae.

To defeat Wace's contention that the tombs were of thirteenth-century construction, Evans drew attention to the stone medallion pithoi found in one of the tombs. They were, he argued, modelled on clay specimens found principally at Knossos. Here they were clearly of Middle Minoan III date. How, then, could a thirteenth-century tomb get furnished with vessels modelled on originals of the seventeenth century? 'The buried magazines of Knossos must in that case have been the scene of expert excavations on the part of the Kings of Mycenae', scoffed Evans.

To support his conclusion that the Medallion Pithoi were of Middle Minoan III date Evans submitted a stratigraphic section relating to the magazine (Fig. 20). The visitor will see that a part of the upper pavement (which incidentally shows the marks of

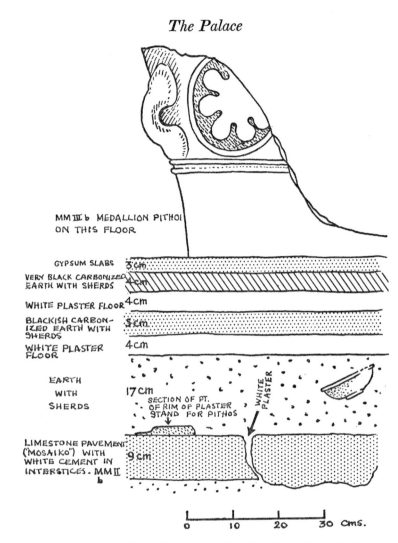

MM III b MEDALLION PITHOI
ON THIS FLOOR

GYPSUM SLABS — 3 cm

VERY BLACK CARBONIZED EARTH WITH SHERDS — 5 cm

WHITE PLASTER FLOOR — 4 cm

BLACKISH CARBONIZED EARTH WITH SHERDS — 5 cm

WHITE PLASTER FLOOR — 4 cm

EARTH WITH SHERDS — 17 cm

SECTION OF PT. OF RIM OF PLASTER STAND FOR PITHOS

WHITE PLASTER

LIMESTONE PAVEMENT ('MOSAIKO') WITH WHITE CEMENT IN INTERSTICES. MM II b — 9 cm

0   10   20   30 Cms.

Fig. 20. Stratigraphic section in the Magazine of the Medallion Pithoi (after Evans's Palace of Minos). A burnt LM II sherd was found below the upper pavement.

intense fire) has been removed, revealing an earlier pavement in which there is a circular base for a jar. Evans reported nothing later than Middle Minoan II sherds from between the two floors, and this implied a Middle Minoan III date for the upper floor. However, once again the find data were incompletely reported.

The Palace

The 1913 notebook has a note on this test which shows that a much burnt piece of Late Minoan II ware was also found under the top pavement.[40] This is consistent with an LM III date for the floor laid over it. Moreover, Evans compared these Medallion Pithoi with one from Magazine X in the West Wing, and there we have already considered the abundant evidence for Late Minoan III pottery beneath the floor. The late date for the bee-hive tombs is now generally accepted by archaeologists; so here, too, there is consistency between the true results from Knossos and those from the Greek mainland. Evans's results confirmed Wace's deductions for Mycenae.

West of the Magazine of the Medallion Pithoi lies another narrow room (Plan I, 57), divided into bays by piers which project from the west wall. These piers have the function of buttresses which prop up the retaining wall of the artificial terrace which forms the Central Court on this side. The piers probably also acted as supports for pillars in a hall above. All this had vanished when excavation started, and the whole area is now roofed in with modern concrete at the level of the Court. When Evans dug there in 1901, he worked his way along the Corridor of the Bays south-wards and emerged on what he later discovered was a landing of the Grand Staircase at the level of the Upper East-West Corridor. It was on this landing that he discovered the large deposit of clay seal impressions mentioned above (see p. 82).

Having emerged from the Corridor of the Bays, we take a few steps left along the East-West Corridor and then turn right through the Verandah of the Royal Guard. This is a gallery overlooking the Hall of the Colonnade, where Evans has set up his restoration of the Shield Fresco, the fragments of which were found (see p. 82) in the staircase to the south of the light-well (Plan I, 35). From this point on we are retracing our steps, but at the level of the upper storey. The top of the Wooden Stairs (reconstructed in stone) is on our right as we pass through the door on the south side of the verandah. Passing the staircase we turn right, and the passage now runs west. On our left is the room above the Queen's Bathroom (Plan I, 40), and next to it is the room above the 'Lair' (Plan I, 36). This square room, when ex-cavated, contained late stirrup-jars of the class LM III B, but

101

Evans called it the Room of the Archives. This was because he conjectured that it had once contained a mass of clay sealings actually found on the upper flight of the Wooden Stairs. His idea was that the 'squatters' or his 'diminished dynasts' had cleared out the archives to make room for the stirrup-jars, and somehow the clay sealings had not only found their way down the stairs but persisted through this late occupation for Evans to find them in 1902. We may recall at this point that some of the stirrup-jars had fallen down over the balustrade of the Queen's Bathroom along with some of the clay sealings (see above, p. 85), while other late stirrup-jars were unearthed standing on the floor in the cupboard below the stairs.

In front of us is the light-well, known as the Court of the Distaffs (Plan I, 37), and flanking it on the south is the Room of the Stone Bench, which lies above the Queen's Toilet Room (Plan I, 38). The small WC in the corner, with its descending shaft discharging into the great drain below, gives us an idea of the elaborate sanitary arrangements in the palace.

7. THE SOUTH-EAST QUARTER[41]

The corridor we have been following, after passing the Room of the Stone Bench, turns left, i.e. east (the route is indicated on Plan I by an arrow with a broken line), and we can look down on the south light-well of the Queen's Megaron. To our right, i.e. south, lies an intricate set of small rooms. Though they are basement rooms, or at any rate on the ground floor, they lie on the level of the upper floor of the Domestic Quarter. This is because we are now about to pass beyond the limits of the great cutting made in the hillside to accommodate the Domestic Quarter.

There has been much reconstruction here, and rooms belonging to different phases of the palace appear side by side. A clue to the puzzle is given by the surviving steps (Plan I, 59). These formed part of a staircase which ascended westwards towards the Central Court. In its upper part it ran over the cupboard which is the room Plan I, 60. West of this is the room Plan I, 61. From its square shape and the remains of gypsum lining slabs found

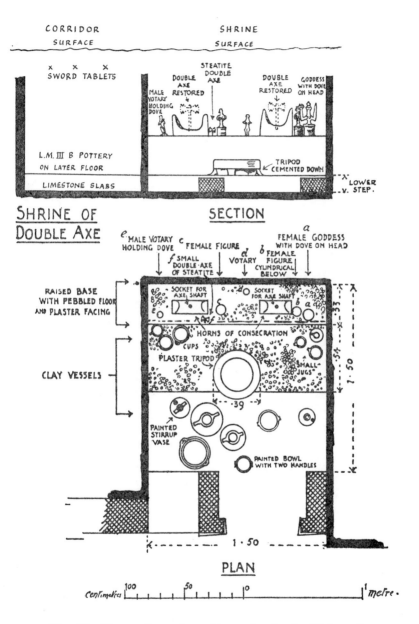

Fig. 21. Plan and stratigraphic section in the Shrine of the Double Axes.

attached to its walls Evans inferred that it was a bathroom. The bath tub at present exhibited there was not found hereabouts.

The 'bathroom' is flanked on two sides by plaster closets. The exterior walls of these chambers are simply thin partitions a bare 4–5 inches thick, comprising a terracotta plaster core covered with a coat of hard red stucco. In these closets was found a fine set of vases including the famous Lily Vases (see below). This set of rooms apparently belonged to an earlier phase of the palace and they had got covered up when the stairs were built above them.

Chief interest in this south-east quarter centres on the little room lying to the south of the plaster closets. This is the Shrine of the Double Axes (Plan I, 64), described by Pendlebury as 'a sad little building, constructed by men of Late Minoan III, after the destruction of the palace'. It was found in its completely furnished state by Evans, although the photograph he published to illustrate it has proved to have been contrived, with different pottery substituted.

The plan with the accompanying section (Fig. 21) gives an idea of its layout, contents, and stratification. The earth cover was a bare metre or less. The shrine is a very small room, about $1\frac{1}{2}$ metres square. On the clay floor a variety of vessels had been left standing, including a late stirrup-jar with the usual conventional octopus decoration. To the north of this area was a raised dais with a pebble floor, in the centre of which was a plaster tripod forming a sort of table of offerings. Immediately behind the dais was a platform running from wall to wall. On this stood two sacral horns and, on either side, a series of painted terracotta figures representing divinities and votaries. They are on exhibition in the Archaeological Museum (see below, p. 125).

All these vessels and furnishings were recognized by Evans as belonging to the Late Minoan III B period. Pottery of the same type was also found in the corridor alongside the shrine. One piece is even attributable to the still later class LM III C (twelfth century B.C.). Above this late pottery, in the 'upper strata' of the corridor, were found Linear B tablets depicting swords (Fig. 22). The find circumstances were such that in 1909 Evans was obliged to date the tablets to the 'period of decadence', and he offered this as evidence for the survival of literacy in this late period. In

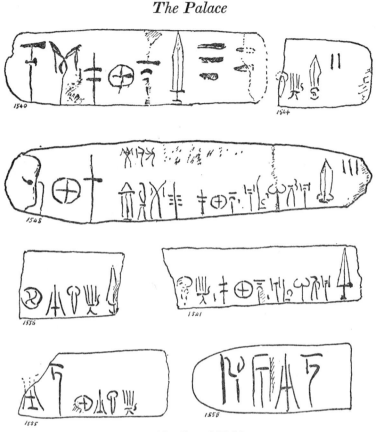

Fig. 22. Sword Tablets.

the *Palace of Minos* however, published some twenty-six years later, he went back on this and reversed the observed stratigraphy, putting the late pots above the tablets.

Along with the tablets was found an important archaeological cross-reference already mentioned (p. 80). Some of the tablets listed men who were designated by the 'man' ideogram. The same ideogram appeared on a clay sealing found with the tablets, and it had evidently sealed the container in which the tablets had been stored. The sealing bore the impress of a seal which had also been used to seal the boxes of arrow heads found in the Arsenal alongside the Royal Road. It would be rather a coincidence if the seal had survived the destruction of the palace and had then been used by the 'squatters' precisely in connection with armaments.

105

The Palace

It is also difficult to imagine 'squatters' with bureaucratic practices, listing craftsmen and stores of bronze swords. On the whole, it would seem simpler to conclude that the official concerned with armaments had been busy in both parts of the palace and that the sealing with its tablets is dated by the pottery found on the floor below it and by the contents of the shrine alongside, as presented in our plan and section.

This south-east quarter was particularly rich in pottery of this late period. Evans first probed it when he was making his preliminary tests in 1900 in order to establish where it was safe to dump his material. One of these spaces was so crammed with late cups resembling handleless Turkish coffee cups that his workmen dubbed it the 'Kapheneion'. Evans also singled out this area as the site of a great mass of the late goblets which he called 'champagne cups'. This mass of late pottery extended northwards as far as the Private Staircase of the Queen's Megaron (Plan I, 33). There it joined up, as we saw, with the great masses of octopus stirrup-jars. These, in their turn, were associated with the deposits of clay sealings and with the Dolphin Fresco (p. 87).

In 1900, when Evans first mentioned the 'Kapheneion' with its accumulation of late cups, he added that 'huge burnt beams also came to light on this side and traces of a vast conflagration'. It would be of interest to know, for the purposes of dating the fire, whether any of the late goblets show signs of burning. Such has proved to be the case, as a recent examination of the material in the Stratigraphic Museum has revealed. The circle of proof is complete. Fig. 21 with its section offers an epitome of the archaeological evidence bearing on this vexed question of Aegean history: when was the palace which housed the Linear B tablets burnt?

At this point, as we leave the palace proper, the visitor may wish to pause and consider the whole 'squatter' story, as propounded by Evans. It is an interpretation of evidence, an instructive example of the way in which an archaeologist seeks to distill history from the sherds which are his main raw material. The factual basis for the story is made up simply of the great quantities of pottery found on the site which was dated by Evans to a period long after the Late Minoan II pottery, considered by him to be characteristic of the palace at the moment of its destruction. We may recall that the sole pieces of such 'Palace Style' pottery found within the palace proper made up only a small fraction of a single vase (see above, p. 39). An eminent authority, long a supporter of Evans, has recently dismissed the 'squatter' hypothesis as a 'myth invented by Evans and Mackenzie'. The plain facts before us are that the Linear B tablets and the accompanying clay sealings were found in the same destruction debris as the late pottery. In any case, the huge quantities of such pottery could hardly have been the possessions of mere 'squatters'.

This difficulty has been recognized by those who still cling to the early dating of the tablets. To explain away the great amount of late pottery an interesting elaboration of the 'squatter' hypothesis has recently been propounded.[42] It is now suggested that the 'squatters' were in fact some priestly body who settled in the ruins after the great fire had destroyed the palace. The site retained its religious associations and a kind of 'ruin cult' had grown up. It was these 'priest-squatters' who stored the large amounts of pottery for sale to pilgrims coming up to worship at the Shrine of the Double Axes, the religious traditions of which persisted. These stores of pilgrim pottery included the very large numbers of octopus stirrup-jars kept in the area of the Queen's Megaron. The double jars found on the earth floor in the Northern Entrance Passage were another such store.

However, there are some difficulties in this new version of the 'squatter' hypothesis. How did the double jars come to be entangled with the great masses of Linear B tablets (see p. 78)? Here in the Corridor of the Sword Tablets the facts are still more recalcitrant. The tablets lay above the late pottery. There is the added difficulty that so much of the late pottery shows the marks of fire, and a straightforward reading of the evidence would associate the burnt tablets with the burnt pottery found with them.

This newly discovered fact has prompted a still subtler refinement of the 'priest-squatter' hypothesis: we are now told that the goblets sold by the 'priest-squatters' had been used 'exceptionally' by their pilgrim customers as incense burners. Hence the marks of burning, which thus had a totally different origin from the marks of burning on the asssociated tablets. However, a re-examination of the said goblets has shown that the marks of burning are found both on the outside and the inside of the goblet cups, on the fractured surfaces of the stems, and even on the underside of the bases. So it would seem simpler to accept the given association of burnt tablets with burnt LM III B pottery. The Shrine with its furniture would then be invaluable evidence for religious worship in the Creto-Mycenaean palace at the moment of its destruction. At this point we may recall yet another archaeological cross-reference. These crude clay idols have been compared with similar material from other late shrines of Crete, e.g. Gournia and Prinias, where they were associated with ritual furniture connected with snake worship. This in its turn showed great similarity to that found in the Snake Room discovered in 1930 deep below the surface of the West Court (see p. 37). The pattern of evidence over the whole palace site is consistent.

The Corridor of the Sword Tablets (Plan I, 65) runs south past the Shrine of the Double Axes. On our left we see another of the sunken 'Baths' (Plan I, 66), or better, Lustral Areas, so characteristic of Minoan architecture. We emerge into a small portico (Plan I, 67) from which we can look down on to some of the houses constructed outside the palace proper. One of them is the House of the Fallen Blocks, so-called from the huge blocks which fell down the slope when this part of the palace collapsed, possibly as the result of an earthquake.

8. The South Front[43]

We now turn right and find ourselves on the South Front. What we see is a line of basements well below the level of the Central Court. Here the hill fell away steeply to the south and a massive terrace wall was built. Parallel to it, at a distance of about eight metres to the south, runs a wall of fine gypsum blocks on a slightly projecting plinth of limestone blocks. This outer line of wall has little or no foundations, and Evans deduced that it had merely supported a flat roof, which formed a verandah at the upper floor level. In between these two lines of walling there are at intervals massive blocks of masonry (shown in broken hatching on Plan I), whose function was to support structures at the upper level between this line and the Central Court to the north. Evans believed that a continuation of the Corridor of the Procession ran along this line. It started at the West Porch (see Plan I) and turned left along the South Front after reaching the south-west corner of the palace. He imagined this east return of the corridor as a portico open on the south side with an open walk along the south half of the corridor. This whole area was particularly rich in finds of Late Minoan III B pottery; but it was the eastern section which we have just reached that yielded an especially suggestive complex of archaeological evidence.

We first take our stand at point 69 of Plan I. Above us, as we look north towards the Central Court, is the replica of the Priest King Fresco which Evans has set up here. Immediately in front of the point where we are standing was a massive block of rubble masonry (Plan I, 75). On the south and east sides of this were found a number of LM III B vessels; further west was a double jar of a type found in abundance in the Northern Entrance Passage along with the Great Deposit of tablets (see above, p. 78). This was in 1900. The following year the area immediately to the north was excavated and produced some remarkable finds, including the fragments of the Priest King Fresco.

Rooms 70 and 71 of Plan I both contained many Late Minoan III B pots, which were carefully described by Mackenzie in his pottery notebook. In Room 71 was also found clear evidence of fire — a jar with burnt beans inside. There was further evidence that a seal cutter had been at work here, for half finished specimens were among the finds. Evans registered this room in the *Palace of Minos* as 'The Lapidary's Workshop of Reoccupation Date'. In Room 72 a great hoard of clay sealings was found, and some of these had been scattered eastwards into Room 73, where they were found in the upper earth along with fragmentary Linear B tablets. Yet other tablets were found further east and north, but always in the upper earth.

In Room 71 the northern half of the floor was found covered with a great heap of burnt wheat. Evans entered this room in his plan likewise as Late Minoan III. It need hardly be stressed that the burnt wheat, like the burnt beans in the adjoining room 70, was clear evidence of a fire at the period indicated by the Late Minoan III B vases found in these rooms.

The Palace

Thanks to Mackenzie's pottery notebooks we now know what evidence in the shape of the all-important pottery finds impelled Evans to attribute the final occupation of these workrooms of the south-east front to 'squatter' artisans. The finds, however, went beyond the dating of just these rooms: they provided a valuable series of archaeological cross-references which link this area with other parts of the palace and so enable us to cross-check the results we have so far surveyed in the tour of the palace.

First, the double jar gives a connection with the Great Deposit of tablets found on the LM III earth floor in the Northern Entrance Passage along with a great number of very similar LM III B jars (see p. 78). The seal impressions found in this area also occur elsewhere. Of outstanding importance were those showing the impress of the 'collared bitch' seal (Fig. 23b), impressions of which recurred in many parts of the palace. In the same year (1901) as these rooms were excavated impressions of the seal were also found in the area to the south of the Throne Room, in the Gallery of the Jewel Fresco. Here they were associated with the Vase Tablets (see above, p. 56 and the section Fig. 6). What is especially intriguing is that along with the Vase Tablets and the 'collared bitch' sealings was found the LM III B strainer which Evans transferred to the Room of the Stirrup-Jars when illustrating his 'decisive evidence' for dating the tablets (see p. 76). Yet another vessel (a stirrup-jar) which figures in that misleading assemblage of evidence was actually found in the area we are now examining. Thus two vessels classified by Evans as LM III B and found in different parts of the palace were closely associated with deposits containing impressions of one and the same seal. Yet other impressions of the 'collared bitch' seal occurred in the Domestic Quarter with its abundant stores of late pottery.

It remains to consider the Priest King Fresco and its find circumstances. Plan I shows that the block of rubble masonry (75) has its east face exactly aligned with the east faces of the west walls of spaces 73 and 74. They evidently belonged to the same structural system. In the centre of this complex of rooms the plan shows the basement walls as especially massive, and some important structure must have existed above them. 73 and 74 would have formed, at the upper level, a narrow elongated corridor. 75

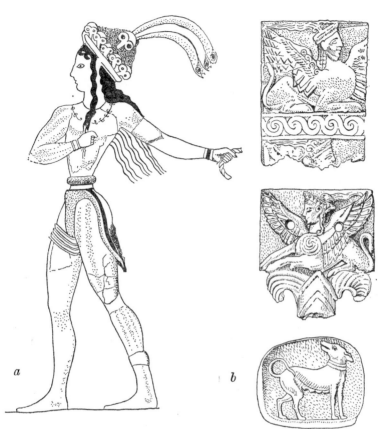

Fig. 23. Finds from the South Front: (a) *the Priest King Fresco;* (b) *the Collared Bitch seal and Sphinxes with plumed headpieces* (*after Evans's* Palace of Minos).

looks like the central support of a staircase with a landing at a point where a T-shaped block of rubble masonry (Plan I, 76) may mark the west wall of the stairs. The vases found to the south of Block 75 were in all probability stored in a cupboard under the stairs.

Evans claimed to have found the fragments of the Priest King Fresco at the foot of the wall of the narrow corridor. In fact they were found at point Plan I, 74, a bare 30 centimetres (11 inches) below the surface, that is in the upper earth, like the clay tablets and sealings. All the pottery observed and recorded in this part of the site was, without exception, of the Late Minoan III B class.

The fresco was found in fragments, and the famous 'Priest King' is Evans's composition. The feathered crown was found separately from the pieces of the human figure, and there is no evidence that it belongs on the head of a man. On the contrary, parallels suggest that a man may have been leading a sphinx, and that the feathered crown belongs to a sphinx and not a man (see Fig. 23).

We now walk along the South Front past the South Propylaeum with its Cupbearer Fresco as far as Rooms 77 and 78 on Plan I. These two are basement rooms with rough rubble walls, and they contained many Late Minoan III B vases. In his notebook for 1901, Evans drew a sketch plan[44] on which he entered the pots with a note 'Bügel [i.e. stirrup-jar] with octopus . . . on floor level and tablets'. At this point, where an association of tablets with a Late Minoan III B vessel is so unequivocally recorded by the excavator, we may recall that below us in the space between the south wall of the palace and the South House (Plan I, 2) Evans reported his most important deposit of what he regarded as Late Minoan II pottery. Much of this, as we saw, has been reclassified as Late Minoan III A, and in any case it was recorded by Mackenzie[45] as thrown out as rubbish during repairs to the palace during the Late Minoan III B period. It is thus evidence for the Penultimate Palace. This pattern of facts is an epitome of the evidence we have observed throughout the site. Finally, we may mention that it was in these rooms that Evans found another of the stirrup-jars which he incorporated in his 'decisive' stratigrahy in the Room of the Stirrup-Jars at the far end of the palace (Plan I, 25).

We now round the south-west corner of the palace, which is strewn with great blocks of stone from the collapsed south foundations. To the west of the West Porch lie considerable remains of buildings with a façade wall constructed of impressive masonry of ashlar blocks on a projecting plinth. At the far west there is a narrow lane, to the west of which runs another wall. In his *Guide*, Pendlebury attributes this complex of buildings to the Middle Minoan III period; 'At this time begins the encroachment on the Palace site of private houses. The south-west wing of the

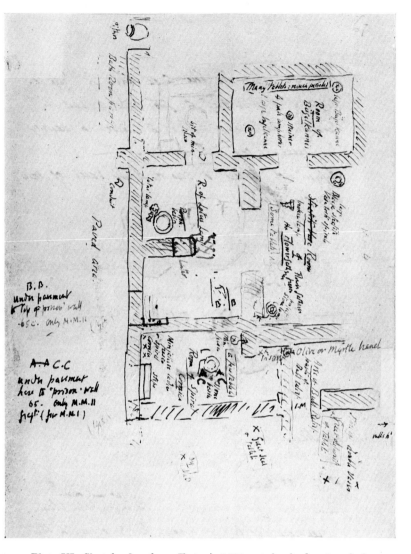

Plate VI. Sketch plan from Evans's 1900 notebook showing finds in the 'Prisons' area. Note: (1) 'Many tablets: much perished' entered alongside the 'Bügelkanne' (stirrup-jar); (2) black steatite vase with spirals along with the Flower Gatherer Fresco; (3) 'miniature ladies fresco and spiral cornice'; (4) 'store of double vases' alongside 'Great deposit of tablets'.

Palace (west of the Corridor of the Procession) is virtually abandoned to some powerful noble'. The building is clearly 'intrusive': it will be seen that to make space for it the massive foundation walls running west from the area of the West Porch were removed. Their jagged ends can be seen at the east end of the building. There is, however, room for doubt about the attribution of its construction to a Middle Minoan III noble. In his 1907 notebook Mackenzie, who excavated the 'lane' referred to above, wrote apropos of its east wall, i.e. the west wall of the house (Plan I, 79): 'There is nothing of the same kind in the Palace that looks so late except the additions to the East Bastion.' As regards the final period of occupation, the same notebook records that the great bulk of the pottery found here was distinctly Late Minoan III B.

Thanks to recent discoveries we can add the testimony of a new witness. An unpublished plan by the architect Fyfe enters the structures in this area west of the Corridor of the Procession as 'walls of period of reoccupation [Late Mycenaean]'. We recall that two of these late walls were actually built in the 'Porter's Lodge' of the south-west entrance to the palace and that close to it was found the Stirrup-Vase Tablet assigned by Evans to the Room of the Stirrup-Jars. Before we return to our starting point, an examination of the elaborate masonry of the north façade of this LM III building may help to dispel possible misconceptions caused by the term 'squatters' with reference to the Creto-Mycenaean period (LM III B).

9. Retrospect and Summary

The tour of this truly labyrinthine palace is now complete, and we return to our starting point in the West Court. From the tangle of evidence a unified picture has emerged. To take stock of the results we stand at point Plan I, 81, opposite the centre of the northern block of magazines, and draw two imaginary sections west-east and north-south through the palace. We are standing on the pavement of the West Court. In this area is the site of the House of the Ducks, where in 1930 Evans found the LM III A material well below the level of the pavement, and also the Snake

Room with its LM III B affinities (see p. 37). To the south is the complex of LM III buildings which we have just visited, while on our left, i.e. north, is the Northwest Treasure House with its double stratification of LM III B over LM II. The famous bronzes were found at the level of the adjacent LM III B floor, while 'Palace Style' vases were found in another of this complex of rooms on the second floor level down (p. 39). Straight in front of us is Magazine XIII, where in 1904 burnt LM III pottery was recovered from the fill of the lower cists (p. 58). Beyond is the pavement of the Long Corridor which again sealed in burnt LM III pottery, recovered in 1903 from the disused cists below the pavement and its clay bedding (p. 57). Beyond is the Throne Room block, where in 1903 and 1913 LM III material was found below the pavement of the Anteroom and underneath the great blocks of the threshold (p. 67). To the north lies the Throne Room Corridor, where at point Plan I, 19 were found the late 'pilgrim flask' and the purple basin alongside the burnt doorposts (p. 64). The whole area to the north of this corridor was drastically rebuilt from the ground floor up in the so-called 'squatter' period (p. 64). Near Plan I, 17 the 'Egyptian Lid' of King Khyan was found in 1901 along with LM III A material in the burnt stratum below the floor of the LM III B room (p. 63).

To the east of the Throne Room lies the Central Court, below the preserved pavement of which at so many points LM III sherds were recovered in test pits sunk between 1904 and 1928. Our west-east section now reaches the East Wing. Here there were such massive concentrations of LM III B material that Evans himself installed his 'dynasts of diminished status', while in 1939 Pendlebury declared that after the great destruction the LM II debris was cleared away and the whole Domestic Quarter re-inhabited with little or no alteration. In the Magazine Plan I, 56 the medallion pithoi resembling the one from Magazine X stood on a pavement that sealed in a much burnt LM II sherd. Finally, at the extreme end of our section there is the East Bastion, the late addition to which Mackenzie compared to the intrusive Southwest House (p. 113).

Our north-south section starts in the Pillar Hall (Plan I, 27), which was built up with late walls when Evans discovered it in

The Palace

1902 (p. 79). Next comes the Northern Entrance Passage, where the great deposit of tablets was inextricably intermingled with LM III B double jars standing on an earth floor which had been laid in the LM III period. Late Minoan II–III material was recovered by Evans himself in 1913 underneath the lower paved floor at point Plan III, 12, while in 1929 Pendlebury found LM II pottery under the foundation of the flanking bastion (p. 77). To the west lies the complex of the rooms again with two LM III floor levels, the Last Palace having been a complete rebuilding from the foundations up. In Room Plan I, 25 Evans sited what has proved to be his wholly fictitious 'decisive' stratigraphy (p. 76). The section now runs through the Central Court with its pavement laid above LM III material and ends in the south in the area of the Priest King Fresco and of Evans's 'Lapidary's Worshop of Reoccupation Date', with the massive deposits of sealings, tablets and LM III B pottery (p. 109). This intricate pattern of archaeological evidence, braced into a rigid structure by its numerous cross-references, and its unity guaranteed further by recent study of the scribal hands of the tablets, requires historical interpretation. If the two commonsense principles used by Evans and his assistants (and, we may add, by the generality of archaeologists) are applied; if pottery found on the floors of rooms indicates final occupation and pottery found underneath floors and inside wall masonry gives a *terminus post quem* for construction; then the only conclusion which the evidence permits is that the Last Palace at Knossos was largely reconstructed when Late Minoan III A and B pottery had already become stratified. It was finally destroyed when the octopus stirrup-jars and the other Late Minoan III B pottery found so abundantly on the site were in use.

This means that the history of the Last Palace at Knossos runs parallel with the 'Palace of Nestor' at Pylos. There the evidence is clear that the building was constructed early in the Late Helladic III B period and destroyed towards the end of that period. In absolute terms this means, on present computations, that the whole history of that palace was played out during the thirteenth century B.C. But archaeologists hold that Late Minoan III B pottery of Crete lasted rather longer than the corresponding

Late Helladic III B of the mainland. It is historically plausible that the destroyers of the Mycenaean civilization, who are believed to have come from the north, stormed and burnt the palaces of the mainland before moving out into the Aegean to capture Crete and Rhodes. Thus Knossos fell later than Pylos.

At all events, what we are surveying from our standpoint in the West Court is the ruins of a Creto-Mycenaean Palace, whose occupants used the Greek language for scribal, administrative and bureaucratic purposes virtually indistinguishable from those of the Mycenaean palaces of the mainland. To match the 'Palace of Nestor' at Pylos we might be tempted to re-christen the Knossian palace after the Cretan hero Idomeneus who took part in the Trojan War; but Nestor was much his senior, and Minos was his grandfather. So 'the Palace of Minos' may without affront to history retain the name which Evans gave it, all the more so, because Minos was a Greek king of Greek legend. What went out of the world on that wild spring day in the twelfth century B.C. was certainly something strange and beautiful: it was an amalgam of Mycenaean Greek and 'Minoan' Cretan cultures.

Appendix

Knossos Exhibits in
the Archaeological Museum

Note: By 'official catalogue' is meant the Guide *by N. Platon. For the new* Guide
by S. Alexiou (1968), at present available only in Greek, see Bibliography.

The exhibits are skilfully arranged in chronological order
so that the visitor as he passes through the rooms will get
an idea of the characteristic products of the main periods
into which the Cretan civilization is classified. The labels Early
Minoan, Middle Minoan, and Late Minoan are not used. Instead
we find a major subdivision into First Palaces (Minoan Proto-
palatial) and New Palaces (Neopalatial Minoan Civilization of
the Three Palaces) preceded by a pre-Palatial Period, which
includes both Neolithic and Early Minoan (see chronological
table on p. 133). The visitor thus passes successively through
rooms devoted to (1) Neolithic and Pre-Palatial Minoan Civilization, (2) Minoan Proto-Palatial Civilization and (3) Neo-Palatial
Civilization of the Three Palaces. Within these rooms the cases
offer a selection of material from the given period arranged
according to places of provenience. Room X is labelled Minoan
Post-Palatial Period 1400–1100 b.c. But here the visitor will in
fact find some of the objects which were closely associated with
the finds of Linear B tablets and clay sealings and so belong to
the Creto-Mycenaean Palace of Knossos. The necessary adjustments to the chronology and to the present lay-out of the Museum
will be indicated room by room and references will be given to the
find-places and circumstances discussed in the body of the book.

ROOM I

Case 1 (three lower shelves) contains neolithic objects from
Knossos. On the top shelf are vases found in a cave sanctuary

117

Appendix

situated a little inland from Amnisos, which was the port of Knossos. The cave was sacred to the goddess Eileithyia, who is mentioned in Homer's *Odyssey* in connection with Odysseus's fictitious visit to Amnisos. References to the goddess (her name occurs in the form Eleuthia) and to Amnisos occur in the Linear B tablets. But it is clear that the religious tradition of the cave sanctuary go back to Neolithic times.

The other cases in this room contain material of this epoch from other Cretan sites.

Room II

Minoan Proto-Palatial Civilization

The construction of the First Palaces is dated in the official catalogue to circa 2000 B.C., but this date has been lowered by some two centuries in some recent computations (see above, p. 33).

Case 25 contains an important find from Knossos which gives us some idea of what Minoan houses looked like. This is the so-called 'Town Mosaic', which was found in the east wing of the Palace. It consists of a number of small faience plaques showing house façades. The original composition may have depicted a whole town with hunting scenes around it or, as Evans believed, a siege scene. The stratigraphy of the find was unclear, but along with the mosaic were retrieved some pieces belonging to the magnificent 'Draughtboard' (see below, Room IV). Thus there is little reason for a chronological separation of the two finds and for dating the mosaic (as in the official catalogue) to 'the third phase of the Proto-Palatial Period (1800–1700)'.

This case also contains specimens of the earliest phase of Cretan script in the shape of prismatic clay bars and small clay labels impressed with pictograms and hieroglyph characters. Those from Knossos were found in the stair cupboard at the north end of the Long Corridor of the Magazines (see p. 62).

Case 24 shows a miniature clay model of a shrine. Notable features are the altar with the double horns and the three columns surmounted by doves.

Appendix

Kamares pottery from Knossos is exhibited in *Cases 22, 23, 27* and *29*. The last contains some larger specimens with decorations in the form of palm trees, garlands and running spirals. Noteworthy are the 'fruit stands' which are a characteristic shape of this period. Some magnificent examples can be seen in the cases devoted to the finds from Phaestos (see Room III).

Room III

This room is devoted to Kamares pottery, mainly from Phaestos. The style owes its name to the cave sanctuary (called after the neighbouring village of Kamares) which can be clearly seen from the Central Court at Phaestos a little below the summit of Mount Ida. It was in this cave that the first specimens of this type of pottery were found. It is notable for the brilliant polychrome decoration with colours which include creamy white, orange and crimson against a black background.

Case 30 shows specimens which were found in the cave. These splendid vases were doubtless brought as offerings to the deity worshipped in this sanctuary.

Room IV

Neo-Palatial Minoan Civilization of the Three Palaces

This room houses material from different palace levels and phases of construction. Notably, the objects bearing Linear A inscriptions do not belong to the Last Palace, i.e. the Creto-Mycenaean Palace, which was distinguished by its great hoards of Linear B inscriptions.

Case 44. The lower shelf has pottery from the beginning of the Neo-palatial period. In the centre is a slender vase with an incised Linear A inscription which was found at Knossos on the South Front. On the middle shelf are cups with ink-written Linear A inscriptions. They come from an early house outside the palace proper on the east side. The find circumstances are in doubt, but some scholars assign them to the Middle Minoan III A period.

Case 45. On the top shelf are the Lily Vases from the 'Plaster Closets' in the Southeast Quarter of the Palace (see above, p. 104).

Appendix

Case 46 shows ritual vessels for use in the cult of the sacred snakes. For the find circumstances and the stylistic comparisons see p. 37.

Case 49. Noteworthy is the small fragment of an altar bearing a Linear A inscription which is exhibited at the extreme right of the bottom shelf. This was found in the House of the Frescoes at Knossos in the vicinity of the Arsenal alongside the Royal Road. The house was, of course, in ruins at the time of the Last Palace.

Case 50. Here are to be seen the faience figures of the Snake Goddess and her companions from the Temple Repositories (see above, p. 55 and Fig. 5). The same deposit also yielded an altar and other ritual furnishings which are exhibited in this case. All these belong to the Penultimate Palace.

Case 51. This contains the famous Bull's Head Rhyton, which was found in the Little Palace in 1908. This type of vase was used for pouring libations, the sacrificial fluid being poured into the vessel through a hole in the top and issuing from a perforation in the lower lip. The rhyton is of black steatite. An interesting feature is the schematical, symmetrical arrangement of the locks of hair, which contrast with the more naturalistic rendering of the hair on the fine specimen from Kato Zakro (Room VIII). The eyes (only one was preserved) were made of rock crystal on which the pupil was painted in bright scarlet and the iris in black. A border of red jasper surrounds the white field of the cornea.

This work of art is dated to the sixteenth century B.C., but the find circumstances are compatible with a much lower date, the thirteenth or even the twelfth century. The Little Palace was in occupation throughout the Late Minoan III B period and its destruction by fire was contemporary with that of the main palace. The box of material associated with the Bull Rhyton, contains Late Minoan III sherds. A bull's head rhyton is depicted on a Linear B tablet from Knossos. Evans attributed it to the West Palace Quarter, but it actually formed part of the Great Deposit of tablets from the Northern Entrance Passage, where it was associated with Late Minoan III B double vases, which we shall see in Room X, Case 138. That, however, such religious objects go back to an earlier date is shown not only by the rhytons from the shaft graves of Mycenae (sixteenth century B.C.) but also by their occurence in representations of Minoan objects in Egyptian tomb pictures of about 1500 B.C. The specimen from Kato Zakro occurred in destruction debris dated by the excavator to circa 1450 B.C.

On the bottom of the base of the Knossos rhyton the Minoan artist has drawn a sketch of the object itself, and this is of importance for the restoration in that it shows the spring of the horns. The present horns of gilded wood are a modern addition modelled on a metal rhyton from Mycenae.

Case 53. Contains bronze vessels — cauldrons, basins, tripods etc. and a huge saw. Some of these objects come from the Northwest Treasure House. For the find circumstances and the association with Late Minoan III B material see above, p. 38.

Case 54. The objects in this case belong to the palace which preceded the Creto-Mycenaean palace of the Linear B tablets. The large vases (note particularly the one with bird decoration) were found in the lower cist of the Temple Repositories (see Plan I, 8 and above, p. 55).

Case 55. Especially noteworthy are two plaques of faience, one showing a cow suckling her calf and the other a wild goat with two kids. These were found in the same deposit as the two divine figures exhibited in Case 50.

Case 56. The ivory figure, apparently of an acrobat in mid-air, was found in the lower stratum of a cupboard below the Wooden Stairs in the Domestic Quarter (see p. 82 and Fig. 15). The figure was not cut from solid ivory, the forearms being attached separately by means of joints and sockets. The hair was rendered by pieces of curling bronze wires on which vestiges of gold plating could be detected. The wires were inserted in tiny holes bored in the head. From its find place this work of art should be assigned to the Penultimate Palace, but there is no evidence which would compel us to date it earlier than the fourteenth century B.C.

Case 57. A gaming board of exquisite workmanship, made from ivory, crystal, faience, lapis lazuli, gold and silver. This, too, belongs to the late Creto-Mycenaean Palace. For the find circumstances see p. 97. The stratigraphy does not support the suggested sixteenth century date.

Case 58. Here are exhibited some of the fine stone ritual vases from the room opening off the Lobby of the Stone Seat (Plan I, 10). For the clear LM III B associations see above, p. 47.

Case 59. Here is the famous Lioness Head Rhyton in carved alabaster — a masterpiece of Creto-Mycenaean art. This was associated with the objects in the previous case and is of the same date.

Around the walls of this room are exhibited a number of larger vessels from the palace. On a corner shelf stands a vase of black steatite with spirals in high relief. For the find position see Evans's sketch plan in his 1900 notebook (Plate VI). It was found above the highest floor level in the Room of the Saffron Gatherer. Thus like the fresco, it belongs to the deposit of the late Creto-Mycenaean Palace. Evans reported it as found on the lowest floor level, and he dated it to Middle Minoan II A, i.e. eighteenth century B.C. (see above, p. 75).

Room V

Passing through the doorway from Room IV we find on the floor to our right the magnificent three-handled alabaster amphora with spirals carved on the rim. This was found in the Sculptor's Workshop in the School Room Area close to the surface above the room containing the *lapis lacedaemonius* which must have been imported from the Peloponnese. That this whole suite of rooms was rebuilt in the Late Minoan III B period was shown above, p. 93. Hence this work of art also belongs to the last days of the Creto-Mycenaean Palace, since the vases were still unfinished.

Case 66 has some fine specimens of stonework including the magnificent flat alabastra which were found on the floor of the Throne Room. As shown above, p. 67, these works of art belong to the final phase of the Creto-Mycenaean Palace which was built when Late Minoan III A:2 pottery had already become stratified below the floor.

Case 62. The bottom shelf shows the Octopus Weight from Magazine XV ('the Great Wool Stone', see p. 62), and the Lotus Lamp from the Area of the Prisons (see p. 69). These, too, belong to the final phase of the Creto-Mycenaean Palace. In the same case is a variety of Egyptian objects, the most important of which

Appendix

is the alabaster lid bearing the name of the Hyksos king Khyan. Another such object is the statuette from the Central Court inscribed with Egyptian hieroglyphs. The official catalogue refers to this as the material on which Minoan chronology has been based: 'in fact they were found in clearly defined levels which received from them an absolute date'. However, on the stratigraphy of these finds see above, p. 18 and 63, where it is shown that the objects were not found in such 'clearly defined levels'.

Case 63. The large decorated strainer exhibited on the middle shelf is of particular interest to the student of Knossos. This object figured, along with two late stirrup-jars, in Evans's stratigraphy which he presented as 'decisive evidence' for dating the Linear B tablets. It was really found in the West Quarter along with the Vase Tablets (see above, p. 56 and Fig. 6). In the *Palace of Minos* (1935) Evans classified this object as Late Minoan III B, and this classification was accepted by the leading authority on Mycenaean pottery, A. Furumark. After its true find place became known various experts have re-classified the piece variously as Late Minoan I–II and Late Minoan III A. The Museum has now separated it from the two stirrup-jars, which we shall see in the Post-Palatial Room.

Case 64. Here are vases recently reconstructed from sherds stored in the Stratigraphical Museum at Knossos. The notice is misleading, since the material does not come from the destruction debris of the Last Palace. Notice particularly the amphoroid krater ('mixing bowl of amphora shape'). This has been reconstituted partly from fragments which were taken from inside the masonry of the spur of wall on the west side of the South Propylaeum. It thus belongs to the Penultimate Palace. For the stratigraphy of this part of the palace see above, p. 51 and Fig. 3b.

Case 61. Alongside the spur of wall just mentioned was found a store of Late Minoan III B jars, and just to the east, above the level of their bases, Evans found in 1900 the piece of porphyry carved with rosettes exhibited on the bottom shelf right. It thus belonged to the debris of the Late Minoan III B Palace, that is the late Creto-Mycenaean Palace. Evans transferred the object to a position below the Middle Minoan III B floor, ascribed it to Middle Minoan III A, and used it as evidence for an early dating of the beehive tombs of Mycenae (see above, p. 51). On the top shelf is a piece of green schist finely carved with half-rosettes. It was found at the back of Magazine XIV. For the find circumstances, which assign it likewise to the Last Palace, see above, p. 62, with Fig. 7b.

Case 69. Contains specimens of the Cretan Linear scripts. Linear A was in use at all Cretan sites; at Knossos it was used until the Penultimate Palace. Linear B was in all probability evolved on the Greek mainland and was brought to Knossos by the Mycenaean invaders. Notable is the greater orderliness in the lay-out of the Linear B tablets as contrasted with those in Linear A, which make a somewhat messy impression. Among the Linear B tablets attention may be drawn to the Great Tablet which was found in the Hall of the Colonnade in the Domestic Quarter (see p. 82 and Fig. 15, 1 for the find circumstances). It contains a list of men's names. A tablet written by the same scribe was found near the Southwest Door in the first days of the excavation (see p. 43). Another tablet of archaeological interest is the small one at the top (right of centre) bearing a red number 93 and a black number 212. The ideograms depict a set of vessels, presumably of bronze, which may be compared with the actual bronze vessels exhibited in Room IV, Case 53. The tablet was found in the Room of the Chariot Tablets in the deposit heaped up against the north foundation wall of the rectangular 'megaron' (see above, p. 46, Plan II, 8 and Fig. 2d). Thus the LM III B associations of the tablet accord with the LM III B associations of the vessels from the Northwest Treasure House.

Room X

We pass through rooms devoted to Cemeteries of the Neo-Palatial Minoan Period, Minoan Neo-Palatial Sites in Central Crete, and Neo-Palatial Minoan Civilization of the Palace of Zakro, to Room X. This is labelled 'Minoan Post-Palatial Period 1400–1100 B.C.' In fact it contains material which is of great importance for the dating of the Creto-Mycenaean Palace at Knossos with its Linear B tablets.

Case 138 (top shelf) presents a selection of the double-jars found on the earth floor along with the Great Deposit of tablets in the Northern Entrance Passage. These vessels are of Late Minoan III B date, as the Museum presents them (see p. 77 and Fig. 14).

Case 131 is of particular archaeological interest. The official catalogue (compiled by Professor N. Platon, formerly Ephor of Crete) comments: 'Some of the most characteristic vases and utensils from the settlements of Knossos (three upper shelves) and Phaestos (lower shelves) belonging to the Postpalatial Period have a clear Mycenaean character. The formerly naturalistic figures of the octopus, cuttle-fish, murex, lily, ivy, etc. are now hardly to be recognized in the very schematic and linear patterns. The vases continue to be varied in shapes and the technique of firing and clay levigation is quite excellent. Most frequent is the stirrup-vase (false-spouted jug), a vessel most suitable for the transport of liquids, the high-stemmed cup, the cylindrical bucket, the vase with concave walls, the pyxis, etc.'

The following items may be picked out. The 'pilgrim flask' with concentric circles exhibited on the top shelf right was found (along with the large porphyry basin now put in the Anteroom to the Throne Room) in the Throne Room Corridor alongside the door with its burnt posts (see p. 64). Pendlebury lists the pilgrim flasks among the new shapes which made their appearance after the destruction of the palace. After the true find place of this vessel became known, various experts have proposed to re-classify it and to update it. The Museum adheres to the classification of Professor Platon.

Alongside the pilgrim flask at the top shelf are two stirrup-jars. One of these is of particular interest because it figured together with the strainer (see above) in Evans's 'decisive stratigraphy' sited in the Room of the Stirrup-Jars. It was, however, actually found on the South Front (see p. 110).

In *Case 130* note particularly the goblets with tall stems which are so characteristic of this late period. Vessels of this type showing marks of severe burning were found in the south-east part of the Palace (see p. 107).

Case 140 contains the clay idols from the Shrine of the Double Axes, and *Case 142* similar objects from Prinias and Gournia (see p. 37).

Appendix

We make our way back to the entrance hall and up the stairs to the first floor. Room XIV is the long hall where Minoan frescoes are exhibited. Others are on view in Rooms XV and XVI. A list follows with the necessary cross-references.

1. The Griffins from the Throne Room. It is widely believed that they were found on either side of the Throne. But this is wrong. For the position and find circumstances see p. 68.

2. The Priest King Fresco, or The Prince of the Lilies. This was found in the surface layer on the South Front. See p. 109.

3. The Bull Relief Fresco from the Northern Entrance Passage. This was found considerably above the LM III B earth floor with its deposits of double-jars and Linear B tablets (see p. 78).

4. The Ladies of the Court or the Ladies in Blue. This spirited composition is the work of Evans's Swiss artist M. Gilliéron, who has assembled it from a few fragments, much smoke-stained, found outside the north wall of the 'Royal Magazines' (i.e. the Area of the Medallion Pithoi, on the stratigraphy of which see pp. 99 f). The heads, together with their elegant coiffure, are entirely the work of Gilliéron.

5. The Dolphin Fresco. This, too, has been composed by Gilliéron from a few fragments. For the clear LM III B associations see above, p. 87.

6. The Toreador Fresco from the Court of the Stone Spout. For the find circumstances, in a court rebuilt towards the end of the Late Minoan III B period, see p. 96.

7. The Shield Fresco. This was found above the upper flight of the Wooden Stairs south of the Hall of the Colonnade (see Fig. 15, 2). The fragments were again few and the composition was guided by the better preserved Shield Fresco from Tiryns (see above, p. 82).

8. The Procession Fresco. This has been likewise reconstructed from very few fragments. Better preserved is the Cupbearer. The provenience is the Corridor of the Procession to the west of the South Propylaeum, see above, p. 43.

9. The Miniature Frescoes (in the official catalogue called

'The Garden Party' and 'Palace Feast'). This came from the area of the 'Prisons' above the floor of the Last Palace which had been built from the foundations up in the Late Minoan III period (see p. 71).

10. La Parisienne. This was found in 1901 in the space behind Magazine XIV where it was associated with the decorated stone carved with half-rosettes (see p. 62, Fig. 7c). In the official catalogue the find year is erroneously given as 1903 and the find place as 'the great six-columned sanctuary hall of the palace', which Evans imagined above this group of magazines.

11. The Spiral Friezes were found in the Area of the 'Prisons' in the same stratigraphic circumstances as the Miniature Frescoes. Like them they belong to the Creto-Mycenaean Palace.

12. The Dancing Girl. Found in the same place and circumstances as the Dolphin Fresco; both belong to the Late Minoan III B period (see above, p. 87).

13. The Saffron Gatherer Fresco. Found above the floor of the Creto-Mycenaean Palace in 1900 in the Area of the 'Prisons' along with the vase of black steatite with spiral relief decorations (see Evans's sketch plan, Plate VI and, for the general find circumstances, p. 75). The Museum shows two restorations side by side; in one the figure is restored as a youth and in the other as a blue monkey.

14. A composition depicting a tri-columnar sanctuary which is believed to represent an architectural feature of the Knossian palace. It comes from the same area as the Miniature Frescoes and like them belongs to the Late Minoan III B period.

All the above frescoes were found within the debris of the Late Creto-Mycenaean Palace, destroyed perhaps as late as the twelfth century B.C. Of earlier date are the specimens from the House of the Frescoes, which lies alongside the Minoan Road, leading west from the Theatral Area (see Plan I). This house also contained an altar bearing an inscription in the Linear A script (see above, p. 120). The most remarkable of the frescoes is the so-called Royal Gardens, showing a landscape with exotic vegetation and animals, including a blue monkey. It was this discovery which prompted the restoration of a blue monkey instead of a youth in the Saffron Gatherer Fresco. From the same house come the fragments, imaginatively restored by Evans as the famous composition called The Captain of the Blacks. However, of the negro 'soldiers' who appear in the reconstruction only the front of a left thigh was found.

Bibliography

A convenient survey of the progress of Aegean archaeology is to be found in A. J. B. Wace and F. H. Stubbings
(eds.), *A Companion to Homer*, 1962, pp. 331–429. E.
Vermeule, *Greece in the Bronze Age* (1964), is among the best
of recent general accounts which restate orthodox views of
Knossos. More stimulating and iconoclastic is J. Alsop, *From the
Silent Earth*, 1964. My own *Mycenaeans and Minoans*, 2nd ed.
1965, argues the account presented in this Guide. On architectural questions the standard work is J. W. Graham, *The Palaces
of Crete*, 1962. J. D. S. Pendlebury, *The Archaeology of Crete*,
1939, despite its date, retains its authority. *A Handbook to the
Palace of Minos at Knossos* by the same author, first published in
1933, was republished in 1954. The new edition includes 'A Survey
of Minoan Civilization' by Sir John Myres and Sir John Forsdyke,
written before the decipherment of Linear B had made its full
impact. *A Guide to the Archaeological Museum of Heraclion* by N.
Platon (2nd ed. 1957) has now been superseded by S. Alexiou
Odigos Arkhaiologikou Mouseiou Irakleiou, 1968, though it retains Platon's historical introduction (see note on p. 117).

P.G.P.K.

Notes

The following abbreviations are used:

AE/NB   The private notebooks of A. J. Evans relating to the Knossos excavations.

BSA   *Annual of the British School at Athens.*

DM/DB   The Day Books of the Knossos Excavations by Duncan Mackenzie.

JHS   *The Journal of Hellenic Studies.*

M & M²   *Mycenaeans and Minoans* (see above).

OKT   *On the Knossos Tablets.* Oxford, 1963.

      I *The Find Places of the Knossos Tablets* by L. R. Palmer.

      II *The Date of the Knossos Tablets* by J. Boardman.

SMK   *A Guide to the Stratigraphical Museum in the Palace at Knossos*, by J. D. S. Pendlebury, 1933–5.

1. This was stated in the first excavation report (*BSA* 6, 1900, 27): 'The Egyptian figure was found ·70 cm. below the surface on the edge of a small remaining patch of pavement.'

2. *AE/NB* 1913. Cf. *OKT* I, Plates XI and XII.

3. See *M & M²*, Chapter VI, pp. 173–219.

4. For an account of the decipherment see J. Chadwick, *The Decipherment of Linear B*, 1958.

5. V. Desborough, *The Last Mycenaeans and their Successors*, 1964, pp. 166 ff.

6. H. W. Catling and A. Millett, 'A Study of the Inscribed Stirrup-Jars from Thebes', *Archaeometry* 8, 1965, 3–85.

7. C. W. Blegen, 'A Chronological Problem', *Minoica*, 1958, 61–6.

8. *M & M²*, pp. 211–9, 223–7. We can now add the testimony of T. Fyfe's measuring book. That none of the pots concerned was

found in the Room of the Stirrup-Jars was established by M. R. Popham, who still adheres to Evans's general position.

9. 'Last Palace and Reoccupation', *Kadmos* 4, 1965, 16–44.

10. *M & M²*, Pt. II.

11. *BSA* 11, 1905, 23.

12. This letter forms part of the Evans papers in the Ashmolean Museum, Oxford.

13. *DM/DB* 1903.

14. *JHS* 23, 1903, 192, Fig. 10.

15. *BSA* 11, 1905, 19 with Fig. 10.

16. *OKT* I, 63–71, 223–6; II, 9–21; *Kretika Khronika* 17, 1963, 290–306; *M & M²*, 263–73.

17. *OKT* I, 79–87, 221–2.

18. *OKT* I, 72–8; II, 21–5; *Kretika Khronika* 17, 1963, 290–306.

19. *Kretika Khronika* 17, 1963, 290–306.

20. It was the 6th pithos found in the first days of the excavation in 1900. Although the vessel was never mentioned in the publications, it appears in plans drawn by all three persons concerned — Evans, Mackenzie and Fyfe.

21. This we know from *DM/DB* 1925.

22. *OKT* I, 88–105, 217–20; II, 32–41.

23. These important findings were established by M. S. F. Hood and communicated in 1964.

24. *M & M²*, pp. 246–56.

25. This observation is also due to M. S. F. Hood.

26. In the Ashmolean Museum, Oxford.

27. *BSA* 6, 1900, 23.

28. *BSA* 7, 1901, 64, Fig. 20.

29. Mackenzie's pottery notebook, 1901, p. 55. For the LM III A:1 classification by M. R. Popham see *OKT* II, 93, n. 5.

30. *OKT* I, 115–29; II, 41, 47.

31. *OKT* I, 111.

32. *OKT* I, 109, 114, 216–7, 245–7; II, 29–32.

33. *J. Raison* in *OKT* I, 247.

34. *SMK*, F I 3; see J. Raison's comment in *OKT* I, 246. The wooden label confirms that the test was carried out in 1903, the handwriting being different from that on the labels which record

the 1913 tests. In 1913 Evans was alone at Knossos and all the labels are inscribed in his hand.

35. *BSA* 6, 1900, 38–40.

36. *OKT* I, 115–29, 209–16, 247–9; II, 41–9; *M & M²*, pp. 213–9, 223–34.

37. *OKT* I, 130–50, 226–8; II, 52–61.

38. Reproduced in *OKT* II, Plate XIV, *b*.

39. *OKT* I, 179–87; II, 51–2; *M & M²*, pp. 234–43.

40. *OKT* I, xi.

41. *OKT* I, 136–7; II, 59–60; *M & M²*, pp. 274–81.

42. M. R. Popham, 'The Last Days of the Palace at Knossos'. *Studies in Mediterranean Archaeology*, vol. V, 1964, pp. 9, 11.

43. *OKT* I, 151–6; 229; II, 9–11.

44. *OKT* I, Pl. XXXI (*a*).

45. *OKT* I, 188–90.

CHRONOLOGICAL TABLE I

CRETE	CHRON-OLOGY	MAINLAND
Neolithic.	Until 3000	Neolithic.
Early Minoan I, II, III = 'Prepalatial'. Bronze age begins.	2700	Early Helladic. Bronze Age begins.
Middle Minoan I and II = 'Protopalatial'. First Palaces. Pictographic, hieroglyphic, and Linear A script. Polychrome pottery.	1900 1800	Middle Helladic. Greeks invade Greece.
Middle Minoan III. Palaces destroyed and rebuilt. 'Neopalatial Period'.	1700 1600	
Late Minoan IA. Knossos secures supremacy in Crete.	---→	Late Helladic I. Start of Minoan influence.
Late Minoan IB. Phaestos destroyed.	1500 ===⋛ ←	Late Helladic II. Increase of Minoan influence. Mycenaean seizure of Crete.
LM II. Knossos only. Greeks at Knossos dominate Crete until LM IIIA:1. Linear B script.	1400	Late Helladic IIIA. Start of Mycenaean expansion in Aegean, etc.
Late Minoan IIIA: 2. Knossos destroyed. Greeks expelled from Crete. Island now purely 'Minoan' and isolated. 'Squatters' at Knossos. Late Minoan IIIB. Mycenaean influences strong.	1375 1300	Late Helladic IIIB. Mycenaean power at its height.
End of LM IIIB. 'Squatters' vanish from Knossos palace site.		End of LH IIIB. Pylos destroyed. Mycenae attacked.
End of Late Minoan IIIC. End of Bronze Age.	1200 1100	Late Helladic IIIC. Final destruction of Mycenae. End of Bronze Age.

——— → = cultural influence.   ———→ = invasion.

	CRETE		MAINLAND
2000	Middle Minoan I–IIIA. First palaces at Knossos and Mallia. Use of the Hieroglyph and Linear A scripts.		
1900			Middle Helladic. LUVIA ARRIVE IN GREECE from Asia Minor ('Grey Minyan foll 'Parnassos Folk'). Connexions Crete only via Cyclades until w end of period.
1800			
1700	Middle Minoan IIIB. The 'New Era'. Rise of second palaces. Knossos and Phaestos royal abodes.		
1600	Late Minoan IA. Dominance of Knossos. Mallia destroyed (Furumark). Phaestos now seat of vassal king.	- - ->	Late Helladic I. COMING THE GREEKS. Rise of Re Power in Argolis. Start of Mino tion.
1500	Late Minoan IB. Artistic hegemony of Knossos. phaestos, Hagia Triada etc. destroyed (Furumark)?	===> - - ->	Late Helladic IIA. Culminatio Minoization. Trade with Aeg opened up at expense of Crete. I of Tholos tombs.
1450	Late Minoan II (Knossos only): the 'Palace Period'. Connexions with Mainland interrupted (Furumark). Destruction of Knossos (and all Cretan cities?). Last Linear A texts.		Late Helladic IIB. Connexion w Crete interrupted. 'The calm be the storm'. Increased penetra of Aegean. Colony established Rhodes (Ialysos). Destruction Minoan colony at Trianda.
1400	Late Minoan III. ARRIVAL OF THE GREEKS, who dominate whole island.	<——	Late Helladic IIIA. Expedi launched against Crete (poss later).
1300	Phaestos and Hagia Triada reoccupied. New settlements under control of Knossos in Western Crete. Knossian pottery 'democratized' and new style influences Mainland. Use of Linear B script.		Late Helladic IIIB. Acme Mycenaean power and expans New dynasty in Pylos. Buildin Palace of Nestor. Use of Linea script. Destruction of Pylos and ho outside palace at Mycenae.
1200	Continuance of Mycenaean power in Central and South Aegean under Cretan influence. Destruction of Knossos by the Dorians.		Late Helladic IIIC. Destruction of Mycenae by Dorians.
1100			

NOTE: The absolute dates are rough approximations, but the dates for Middle Minoan may The status of Late Minoan II (Palace style) is contested.- - -> denotes 'cultural influen

TROY	EGYPT	
	Dynasties XII–XIII	2000
TROY V		
		1900
TROY VI		
ably occupied by Anatolian people		
king a language akin to the Luvian		1800
e 'Parnassos Folk'.		
		1700
	Hyksos in Egypt	
		1600
	Dynasty XVIII	
		1500
		1450
		1400
		1300
TROY VIIA	Dynasty XIX	
royed by Mycenean Greek expedi-		
		1200
TROY VIIB	Dynasty XX	
		1100

300 years too high (Åström and Levi). Late Minoan IA and IB are probably contemporary.
→denotes 'invasion'.

Plan I. Plan of the Palace at Knossos after Evans's *Palace of Minos*, revised in the light of the excavation records and an unpublished plan by Theodore Fyfe). (1) South-West Door (p. 43); (2) LM II sherds (p. 43); (3) and (4) LM III B jars (p. 44); (5) reconstructed stairway (p. 44); (6) point from which photograph of Plate I was taken; (7) Room of the Tall Pithos (p. 55); (8) Temple Repositories (p. 55); (9) East Pillar Room; (10) West Pillar Room; (11) point in Long Corridor of the Magazines crossed by the section Fig. 5 (p. 56); (12) blocking wall removed in 1901 (p. 56); (13) Linear B tablets (p. 62); (14) stairs below which hieroglyphic tablets found (p. 63); (15) North Bath or Lustral Area (p. 63); (16) North Portico (p. 63); (17) locality of the Egyptian Lid (p. 63); (18) corridor of the North-West Magazines (p. 64); (19) door in Corridor of the Stone Basin (p. 64); (20) Anteroom to the Throne Room (p. 66); (21) Throne Room (p. 66); (22) LM III sherds found below pavement of Central Court (p. 69); (23) Room of the Lotus Lamp (p. 69); (24) Room of the Saffron Gatherer (p. 75); (25) Room of the Stirrup-Jars (p. 76); (26) point of Northern Entrance Passage where test pit of 1913 made (p. 77); (27) Hall of the Eleven Pillars (p. 79); (28) Theatral Area (p. 79); (29) Grand Staircase (p. 80); (30) Hall of the Colonnade (p. 81); (31) Hall of the Double Axes (p. 88); (32) East–West Corridor (p. 82); (33) Queen's Megaron (p. 84); (34) Shield Fresco (p. 82); (35) Wooden Stairs (p. 82); (36) the 'Lair' (p. 84); (37) Court of the Distaffs (p. 84); (38) Queen's Toilette (p. 84); (39) Corridor of the Painted Pithos (p. 84); (40) Queen's Bathroom (p. 85); (41) east light-well of Queen's Megaron (p. 85); (42) south light-well of Hall of Double Axes (p. 89); (43) East Stairs (p. 90); (44) first tablets found in 1901 (p. 92); (45) Room of the Posts (p. 92); (46) LM III B blocking wall forming magazine (p. 93); (47) Sculptor's Workshop with stone amphoras (p. 93); (48) School Room with (49) magazine (p. 95); (50) Court of the Stone Spout (p. 95); (51) Magazine of the Giant Pithoi (p. 97); (52) Corridor of the Draughtboard (p. 97); (53) North-East Hall (p. 98); (54) North-East Magazines (p. 98); (55) Room of the Oil Press (p. 99); (56) Magazine of the Medallion Pithoi (p. 99); (57) Corridor of the Bays (p. 101); (58) deposit of clay sealings (p. 101); (59) stairs (p. 102); (60) bathroom (p. 104); (61) Plaster Closet (p. 104); (62) large deposit of LM III cups (p. 106); (63) Plaster Closet (p. 104); (64) Shrine of the Double Axes with (65) Corridor of the Sword tablets (p. 104); (66) South-East Bath (p. 108); (67) reconstructed portico (p. 108); (68) Priest King Fresco (p. 110); (69) South Corridor (p. 108); (70) Lapidary's Workshop of Reoccupation Date, also Area of Beans (p. 109); (71) Area of Burnt Wheat (p. 109); (72) Room of Clay Seals (p. 109); (73) Room of the Clay Signet (p. 109); (74) find place of Priest King Fresco (p. 111); (75) rubble block, perhaps centre pier of stairs (p. 111); (76) rubble block perhaps marking landing of stairs (p. 111); (77) and (78) Rooms of the Vases *in situ* (p. 112); (79) South-West House (p. 112); (80) test-pit of 1901 (p. 34); (81) see p. 113.

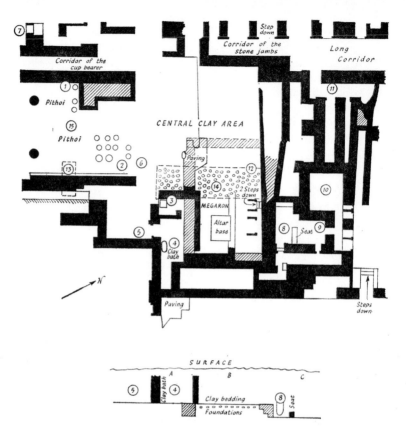

Plan II. The South Propylaeum Area (see pp. 41–55). The black walls are the actual walls of the Last Palace system as surveyed by Evans's architect Theodore Fyfe. The hatched rectangle represents the foundations of the 'megaron' discovered in 1907. The section shows the stratigraphy of the tablets in the Clay Bath and of the Chariot Tablets found close to the north side of the 'megaron' foundations. (1) and (2) the first LM III B pithoi; (3) bronze statuette found between walls constructed at a late stage of the 'reoccupation' but stated by Evans to have been found in a Middle Minoan environment. These late walls of the 'bathroom' and its inner recess represent the last of three architectural phases of the Palace. The north wall overlay the foundation of the 'megaron', which in its turn overlay the foundations of the former stair bastion (14). (4) Pithos no. 6, found alongside the clay bath, unreported by Evans; (5) 'tea set' found in the burnt remains of a shelf well above the level of the base of pithos 6; (6) the first Linear B tablet found along with a LM III B stirrup-jar. (7) South-West Door with the tablet written in the same hand as the Great Tablet from the Domestic Quarter (see p. 43); (8) deposit of Chariot Tablets, which reached as far as (9), later sited by Evans in a cupboard under stairs constructed by him. (10) Room of the Stone Vases including the Lioness Head Rhyton (see p. 47). (11) Corridor of the House Tablets; (12) a stone lamp representing the furthest point of scatter of the vessels from room (10). (13) Concealed cist, discovered in 1925, underlying the east wall of the Propylaeum; LM III sherds were among those recovered from the fill of the cist. (14) Foundation of the east stair-bastion. (15) Piece of carved stone rosettes found in 1900 between the LM III B jars some 20 cm above their bases; in his attack on Wace Evans stated he had found it below the Middle Minoan III B floor.

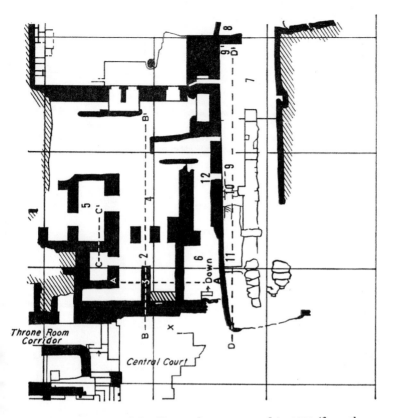

Plan III. The Area of the 'Prisons' as excavated in 1900 (from the excavation report of 1900). For the sections A—A¹, B—B¹, C—C¹, D—D¹ see Figs. 10, 12, 13 and 14. (1) North foundation of the North wall of the Room of the Lotus Lamp over steps originally descending to the floor of the Penultimate Palace; (2) Room of the Lotus Lamp; (3) late wall built of re-used materials and resting on a wall of the 'Prisons'; (4) Room of the Saffron Gatherer; (5) Room of the Stirrup-Jars; (6) Room of the Spiral Cornice; (8) late wall resting on the LM III earth floor; (9—9¹) Great Deposit of tablets; (10) 'Great Seal' with tablets near surface; (11) surface deposit of tablets.

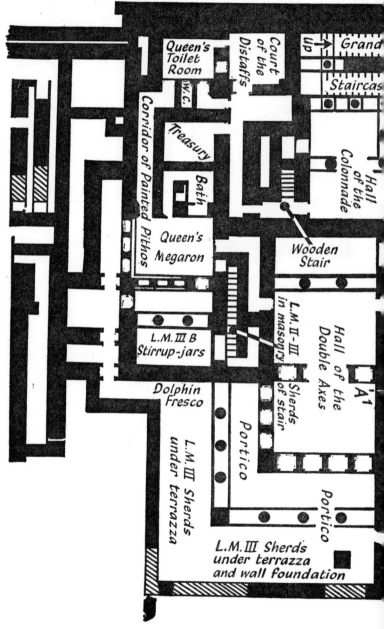

Queen's
Toilet
Room

Court
of the
Distaffs

Up →   Grand

Staircas

W.C.

Treasury

Bath

Corridor of Painted Pithos

Hall
of the
Colonnade

Wooden
Stair

Queen's
Megaron

L.M. II-III
in masonry
of stair

L.M. III B
Stirrup-jars

Hall of the
Double Axes

A'

Dolphin
Fresco

L.M. II-III
Sherds
of stair

Portico

L.M. III Sherds
under terrazza

Portico

L.M. III Sherds
under terrazza
and wall foundation

Portico

Plan IV. The Dom

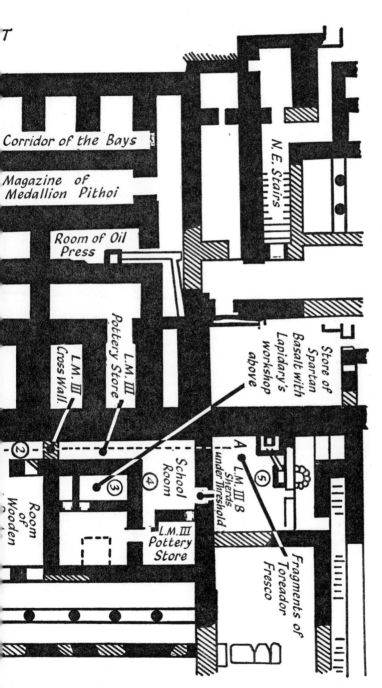

Corridor of the Bays

Magazine of Medallion Pithoi

Room of Oil Press

N.E. Stairs

Pottery Store

L.M. III

L.M. III Cross Wall

Store of Spartan Basalt with Lapidary's workshop above

②

③

④

School Room

Ⓐ L.M. III B Sherds under Threshold

⑤

Room of Wooden

L.M. III Pottery Store

Fragments of Toreador Fresco

ter (see pp. 80–102).

Index

Index

Index